Trump Talks

P. D. Payne

ISBN: 1983600792
ISBN-13: 978-1983600791

DEDICATION

This book is dedicated to the American people.

CONTENTS

ACKNOWLEDGMENTS

I am thankful to all the faithful public servants who strive to keep our great country operating smoothly, for lovers of country everywhere, of any political party, who believes in our great experiment.

Introduction

It is probably an understatement to claim that the Trump presidency is like no other former presidency. The way Trump communicates, the way he thinks, the way he speaks: the American people have never seen anything like it.

President Trump often wages battle against what he calls "fake news." While it is sometimes the case that the news media allows its own biases to color the truth of the current presidential administration, it is more often true that Trump, and his spokespeople, use the term "fake news" to distract the public's attention from serious gaffes and mishaps.

In the midst of bipartisan bickering, perhaps it is more important than ever to record the actual words the president uses. By focusing on the president's own words, biases can at least be reduced.

Having a collection of Trump's own words all in one volume also allows one to easily check the facts. It is especially important when one is dealing with a president who seems to go back and forth and even deny the things he himself has said.

In this volume, the reader will find the most important presidential speeches of 2017, including the now infamous Charlottesville infrastructure speech in which the president blamed "both sides," as well as one of Trump's most well-known rally transcripts from August 2017. I have included the rally transcript because it shows the difference of content and tone when the president speaks for himself rather than with the words of a speech writer.

It is my hope that, by compiling this volume of the president's own words, a more civil, focused conversation among those who disagree politically may arise.

Sincerely,

P.D. Payne

Remarks by President Trump at Tax Reform Event

This is a transcript of the president's remarks, which took place at the Indiana Farm Bureau Building.

THE PRESIDENT: Thank you very much. You just want massive tax cuts. That's what you want. That's the only reason you're going so wild. (Applause.)

But it's wonderful to be back in the great state of Indiana. What a place. (Applause.)

I want to thank Senator Todd Young, Senator Joe Donnelly, Representative Jackie Walorski, Representative Susan Brooks, and Representative Mike [sic] Messer for joining us today. Thank you very much. Thank you very much for being here. Appreciate it. (Applause.)

I also want to thank members of my economic team, Secretary Steven Mnuchin and Director Gary Cohn, for joining us, as well. We appreciate it. (Applause.)

Let me begin by saying that our hearts and prayers go out to the people of Puerto Rico and the Virgin Islands who are suffering in the wake of yet another catastrophic hurricane. I mean, their island was virtually destroyed. Federal agencies are working closely with local partners to help these communities get back on their feet as soon as possible.

Texas, Florida, and Louisiana are doing great, and the recovery process is happening very, very quickly.

I will be going down to Puerto Rico next week to get an on-the-ground briefing about the disaster recovery and to see all of our great first responders and to meet a lot of the people who were so affected by these storms. We are with you now, I tell them, and we will be there every step of the way until this job is done. It is truly catastrophic what happened in Puerto Rico. (Applause.)

And massive amounts of water, food, and supplies, by the way, are being delivered on an hourly basis. It's something that nobody has ever seen before from this country, I can tell you that. And I'm very proud of all of the folks that have worked so hard in FEMA, all of our first responders, all of our police that have gone to the island because their police force has been so badly affected. And many of their policemen — in fact, most of the police people have lost their homes, and it's been a tough go. But we are — we're going to get it back.

Before we go on to discuss the largest tax cut in our county's history, I also want to provide a brief update on healthcare. We have the votes on Graham-Cassidy. But with the rules of reconciliation, we're up against a deadline of Friday — two days. That's just two days. And yes-vote senator — we have a wonderful senator, great, great senator — who is a yes vote, but he's home recovering from a pretty tough situation. And with so many great features, including all of the block granting, the money to the states, et cetera, et cetera, our healthcare plan is really going to be something excellent. It's going to be better managed for the people that it serves. Having local healthcare representatives is far better than having healthcare managed from Washington, D.C. Not even a contest. (Applause.)

And many, many governors, as you also see, have agreed with us and approved it and really look forward to running it properly. But again, because the reconciliation window is about to close, we have to wait a few months until it reopens before we take a vote. So we're getting all of the good signs from Alaska and the others to repeal and replace Obamacare. And I was hoping this would be put on my desk right after we won the election, and I'd come in and sign. But it didn't work that way. There were a couple of people that — I won't say anything. (Laughter.) But early next year when reconciliation kicks back in, in any event long before the November election, we're going to have a vote. And we're going to be able to get that through, and I think we'll actually get it through very easily and the time makes it easier.

But speaking of reconciliation, the Republican Senate needs to get rid of the filibuster rule, which is blocking so many great legislative reforms the American people badly want and deserve. By the way, the Democrats, if they had the opportunity, which hopefully they won't for many, many years, they would get rid of it on day one. And most of you know exactly what I'm talking about.

We're here today in Indiana to announce our framework to deliver historic tax relief to the American People. (Applause.)

This is a once-in-a-generation opportunity, and I guess it's probably something I can say that I'm very good at. I've been waiting for this for a long time. We're going to cut taxes for the middle class, make the tax code simpler and more fair for everyday Americans, and we are going to bring back the jobs and wealth that have left our country — and most people thought left our country for good. (Applause.)

We want tax reform that is pro-growth, pro-jobs, pro-worker, pro-family, and, yes, tax reform that is pro-American. (Applause.) It's time to take care of our people, to rebuild our nation, and to fight for our great American workers. (Applause.)

Indiana is a tremendous example of the prosperity that is unleashed when we cut taxes and set free the dreams of our citizens. This state has claimed a powerful competitive edge built on low taxes and less regulation — and are we cutting regulation? (Applause.)

And businesses all across the country have taken notice. In recent years, Indiana has welcomed dozens of companies fleeing high taxes and high-tax states. Thousands of new jobs and massive capital investment have followed — meaning a better quality of life for the people of Indiana.

All of this is possible because the people of this state have made a decision. They chose to make Indiana competitive again. They chose, and their choice was so important. It included electing a governor, who you may have heard of — (laughter) — who signed the largest income tax cut in the state's history, our very, very terrific person and terrific Vice President, Mike Pence. (Applause.)

It's time for Washington to learn from the wisdom of Indiana. We need Washington to promote American jobs instead of obstructing them. That is what I have been working to achieve every day since I took office. That is what I talked about on the campaign trail.

Already, we're seeing the results of an economic policy that finally puts America first. (Applause.) Unemployment is at a 16-year low. Unemployment for African Americans is near its lowest point since the turn of the millennium. It's really a fantastic thing to see. (Applause.)

Wages are rising. Optimism among manufacturers has reached all-time highs. GDP growth last quarter reached 3 percent way ahead of schedule; nobody thought that was going to happen for a long time. (Applause.) And this quarter, I believe, would have been better, but the hurricanes will have an impact. But other than that, it would have been, in my opinion, even better.

Your government is working for you once again, not for the donors, not the special interests, but the hardworking taxpaying citizens of our country. (Applause.)

America is back on the right track. And I see so many red hats — Make America Great Again. That's what we're doing — Make America Great Again. (Applause.) But our country and our economy cannot take off like they should unless we dramatically reform America's outdated, complex, and extremely burdensome tax code. It's a relic. We've got to change it. We have to compete — compete with other countries.

The current tax system is a colossal barrier standing in the way of America's economic comeback because it can be far greater than it's ever been. But we're going to remove that barrier to create the tax system our people finally, finally, finally — and want and deserve.

For several months, my administration has been working closely with Congress to develop a framework for tax reform. Over the next few months, the House and Senate will build on this framework and produce legislation that will deliver more jobs, higher pay, and lower taxes for middle-class families — for the working man and woman — and for businesses of all sizes. I look forward — (Applause.) Thank you.

I look forward to working with Congress to deliver these historic tax cuts and reforms to the American people. These tax cuts are significant. There's never been tax cuts like what we're talking about.

Our framework is based on four key ideas: First, we will cut taxes for the everyday, hardworking Americans — the people that work so long, so hard, and they've been forgotten. But they're not forgotten anymore. I think we proved that on November 8th. (Applause.)

Under this framework, the first $12,000 of income earned by a single individual will be tax free, — (applause) — and a married couple won't pay a dime in taxes on their first $24,000 of income. So, a married couple — up to $24,000 — can spend their money on their family, on their children, on what they have to do. So much better.

In other words, more income for more people will be taxed at a rate of zero. (Applause.) At this zero percent rate, taxable income will be subject to just three tax rates of 12 percent, 25 percent, and 35 percent.

Jonathan Blanton and his wife Jamie from Greentown are here with us today. Where are they? Oh, hello, Jonathan. How are you? (Applause.)

Jonathan does industrial janitorial work and Jamie works at an auto company. Together they're raising four beautiful children, and last year they earned less than $90,000. Under our tax plan they would have saved more than $1,000, and it could be substantially more. And that's just on federal taxes. So they would have saved at least $1,000.

Middle-income families will save even more money with an increased child tax credit for children under the age of 17, which so many families have been calling for. (Applause.)

We will eliminate the marriage penalty in the existing credit and expand eligibility to include even more middle-income families. Greatly expanded.

We're also expanding the child tax credit because we believe the most important investment our country can make is in our children. (Applause.) And this is just one more critical way that we're targeting relief to working families.

In addition, under our framework, those caring for the elderly loved — and we love these people, but we're caring, and we take such care of the elderly and other adult dependents — will receive financial relief in the form of a $500 tax credit. (Applause.)

We're doing everything we can to reduce the tax burden on you and your family. By eliminating tax breaks and loopholes, we will ensure that the benefits are focused on the middle class, the working men and women, not the highest-income earners. (Applause.)

Our framework includes our explicit commitment that tax reform will protect low-income and middle-income households, not the wealthy and well-connected. They can call me all they want. It's not going to help. I'm doing the right thing, and it's not good for me. Believe me. (Applause.)

But what is good for me — not only as President and legacy — what is good for me is if everything takes off like a rocket ship, like it should have for 20 years. That's good for me. That's good for everyone. (Applause.) And that's what I think is going to happen. (Applause.) And a lot of very wealthy people feel the same way, believe me.

In fact, we are eliminating most itemized deductions that primarily benefit the wealthiest taxpayers. We've also given Congress the flexibility to add an additional top rate on the very highest income earners to provide even more tax relief for working people.

Second, our framework will make the tax code simple, fair, and easy to understand, finally. (Applause.)

Americans waste money. Americans waste so much money — billions and billions of dollars and many hours each year to comply with our ridiculously complex tax code. More than 90 percent of Americans use assistance to prepare their taxes. Under our framework, the vast majority of families will be able to file their taxes on a single sheet of paper. (Applause.)

We are also repealing the alternative minimum tax, or AMT. About time. (Applause.)

The AMT is actually a shadow tax system that requires many people to calculate their taxes two different ways and pay the higher of the two amounts. You're all familiar with it. Under our framework, the AMT will make even less sense because we are repealing many of the special interest tax breaks that it was designed to deal with. We are making our taxes simple again. We are simplifying our tax system.

To protect millions of small businesses and the American farmer, we are finally ending the crushing, the horrible, the unfair estate tax, or as it is often referred to, the death tax. (Applause.)

That means, especially for all of you with small businesses that are really tremendous businesses, you'll be able to leave them to your family, and your family won't have to run out and do a fire sale to try and get the money to pay the tax — lose the business, ends up going out of business. All of those jobs are lost. The farmers in particular are affected. They have wonderful farms, but they can't pay the tax, so they have to sell the farm. The people that buy it don't run it with love. They can't run it the same way, and it goes out. So that death tax is a disaster for this country and a disaster for so many small businesses and farmers. And we're getting rid of it. (Applause.)

Now if you don't like your family, it won't matter, okay? (Laughter.) But for those that love your family, it matters a lot. (Laughter.)

With us today is Kip Tom, a family farmer from Leesburg — Where's Kip? Go ahead, Kip. Hi, Kip — (applause) — who fears that his family's farming heritage — it's been a long time. How long, Kip? A hundred and eighty-seven years — that's peanuts, Kip. (Applause.) Wow. That's a long time. But that great heritage could come to an end because of the death tax, or the estate tax, and could make it impossible for him to pass that legacy to his wonderful family. We're not going to let that happen.

We are not going to allow the death tax to steal away the American Dream from these great, great families, many of which are in this room today. (Applause.)

We will protect our farmers, our ranchers, and our small businesses, and we will make taxes simple, easy, and fair for all Americans. Okay? (Applause.)

Third, we will cut taxes on American businesses to restore our competitive edge and create more jobs and higher wages for American workers. (Applause.)

In Indiana, you have seen firsthand that cutting taxes on businesses makes your state more competitive and leads to more jobs and higher paychecks for your workers. Now, we want to do the same thing for America, making our country more competitive with other nations. And in many cases, those other nations are taking advantage of us in so many ways. They say they're friends, and perhaps they are, but believe me, I am renegotiating our trade deals, including NAFTA, including many other trade deals. (Applause.)

And through regulation, all you have to do is look at the massive pipelines — Dakota Access. You take a look, 48,000 jobs immediately approved. So we're letting that happen.

But in terms of the tax and the tax strategy that Ronald Reagan used to create an economic boom in the 1980s: When our economy took off, the middle class thrived, and the family income of all families was increasing more and more. And it was a beautiful sight to behold.

Since then, other nations have adopted, unfortunately, our playbook and ran it even better than we did. And I shouldn't say even better because we didn't run it well at all, and we let other nations come in and take advantage of us and take our jobs away and take our businesses out. And we're stopping that, and you see it right here what we've done.

Today, our total business tax rate is 60 percent higher than our average foreign competitor in the developed world. That's not good. We have surrendered our competitive edge to other countries, but we're not surrendering anymore. We're not surrendering anymore.

Under our framework, we will dramatically cut the business tax rate so that American companies and American workers can beat our foreign competitors and start winning again. (Applause.) We will reduce the corporate tax rate to no higher than 20 percent. That's way down from 35 and 39 — (applause) — which is substantially below the average of other industrialized nations. This is a revolutionary change, and the biggest winners will be the everyday American workers as jobs start pouring into our country, as companies start competing for American labor, and as wages start going up at levels that you haven't seen in many years. (Applause.)

When our companies move to other countries, it's our loyal American workers who get hurt. And when companies stay in America, and come to America, it's our wonderful workers who reap the rewards.

And I just left the United Nations last week, and I was told by one of the most powerful leaders of the world that they're going to be announcing, in the not-too-distant future, five major factories in the United States — between increasing and new — five. (Applause.) You'll be hearing about that very soon.

And I said thank you very much, and he said, "you know what? It's starting to happen in the United States. It's starting to happen." So I just wanted to let you know that. I promised I wouldn't say who. I'll keep my word. Okay? (Laughter.) Unless you force me. (Laughter.)

AUDIENCE MEMBERS: Who?

THE PRESIDENT: Members of both parties — it happens to be in the automobile industry. That's a good industry. (Laughter.) Members of both parties should agree that we need a tax code that keeps jobs in our country and brings jobs back to our country. (Applause.)

And for the millions of small businesses and farms that file their taxes as sole proprietors, S corporations or partnerships, we will cap the tax rate they pay at 25 percent — much lower. Big difference. (Applause.) This will be the lowest top marginal income tax rate for small and mid-size businesses in this country in more than 80 years. (Applause.)

To give businesses even more reason to boost their investment in America, for the next five years, our framework will allow to fully write off — listen to this — the cost of equipment in the year they buy it. That is big. (Applause.) And that's instead of having to take deductions and deduct the cost over a long period of time. Now that's called incentive. That's called incentive. (Applause.) This will be tremendously important to help American businesses afford the heavy industrial machinery and other capital investments they need to grow big and grow strong.

Joining us today is John Gannon, the owner of a custom wood fencing and deck construction company in Indianapolis. John is the father of nine children, and recently celebrated his 35th wedding anniversary. Congratulations, John. (Applause.)

And John is in the fencing company, as you heard, and I'm just thinking — I have to mention this — you know, we have a fence around the White House. (Laughter.) We have a fence around the White House, and they want to build a new fence. And I figured, you know — I'm pretty good at construction — I figured, I don't know, maybe a million, maybe a million-and-a-half. And this has been taking place over a long period of time — previous administrations.

So I said, "how much is the fence you're talking around the White House?" "Sir, the fence will cost approximately $50 million." I said, "What?" (Laughter.) I kid you not, and we have thousands of things like that. Thousands. We're going to get it all down, but think of that: $50 million. Now, I assume it's a strong fence. (Laughter.) Okay? So, John, do you think you could do it for slightly less than $50 million? I think he could take $49 off right now and he'd have plenty of profit. Right? Right, John? It's crazy. (Applause.) It's crazy. Never understand it, but we're working on it.

John says that a tax cut like we're proposing will make his business more competitive, allowing him to expand, hire more workers, and raise wages for his current employees. Right, John?

Also with us is Aaron Williams, a father of two who works in the field of information technology. Where's Aaron? Hello, Aaron. Hi. (Applause.) It's a good field.

Aaron has seen the disastrous effects of high — and just literally, high corporate tax rates right up close and personal, as more and more high-tech jobs are shipped overseas. You've been watching it, Aaron. Right? All over. Like millions of other Americans, Aaron wants to bring those jobs back to the United States.

We're going to reduce the tax rate on American businesses so they can keep jobs in America, Aaron; create jobs in America; compete for workers in America; and raise wages right here in America. You're going to be in a much different position. Okay? (Applause.) Thank you. Tremendous incentives.

We want more products proudly stamped with those four beautiful words: Made in the USA. Right? (Applause.) Made in the USA.

Finally, our framework encourages American companies to bring back the trillions and trillions of dollars in wealth that's parked overseas. Our current tax system — (applause) — trillions. And by the way, for years I've been hearing it's 2.5 trillion. So I've been hearing this for about five years, so I assume it's much more. Right? But Democrats want to do it, and Republicans want to do it. For years — who doesn't want to do it? They want to bring — but they can't do it because it's so restrictive, and the taxes are so ridiculous. So they can't do it. So the money stays in other countries, and it's invested in other countries. We want to bring it back.

But think of it, it's one of the few things — Democrats want it and Republicans want it. So they both want it, and yet for years they haven't been able to do it. Now we're doing it. We're doing things. (Applause.)

You know, it's one thing when we want a healthcare and they want a healthcare, and there's a dispute. But here's something everybody wants and they can't do it. So you can tell you, there's a broken system in D.C., but we're getting it fixed rather — I think — rather rapidly. You'll be seeing that over the next few months.

Our current tax system makes us one of the few developed nations in the world to punish our companies when they bring wealth earned overseas back into our country. We're punishing them for bringing the money back in.

As a result, corporations have parked many trillions of dollars in foreign countries, and many have incorporated abroad in order to avoid our punitive tax system altogether. And some companies actually leave our country because they have so much money overseas — so much, it's an incredible amount — that they move the company to get their money. We're going to let them bring the money back home. (Applause.)

Our framework will stop punishing companies for keeping their headquarters in the United States. We're punishing companies under our codes for being in the United States. We will impose a one-time low tax on returning money that is already offshore so that it can be brought back home to America where it belongs and where it can be put to work and work and work. (Applause.)

The framework I've just described represents a once-in-a-generation opportunity to reduce taxes, rebuild our economy, and restore America's competitive edge. Finally. (Applause.)

And I have to say, just before coming here we released some of the details of the tax and the tax reform and the tax cuts, and it has really received tremendous, tremendous reviews. And if Senator Donnelly doesn't approve it, because you know he's on the other side, we will come here. We will campaign against him like you wouldn't believe. (Applause.) I think they're going to approve it. I think we'll have — actually, I think we'll have numerous Democrats come across because it's the right thing to do.

These reforms will be a dramatic change from a failed tax system that encourages American businesses to ship jobs to foreign countries that have much lower tax rates. It's what we can't do. Our competitors have much lower tax rates. But no longer. My administration strongly rejects this offshoring model, and we have embraced the new model. It's called — the American model. (Applause.)

Under the American model, we are reducing burdens on our businesses as long as they do business in our country. That's what we want. We want them to do business in our country, not to leave our country like a number of firms from Indiana. Some made some great promises to me, but those promises are only being partially kept because they're incentivized to leave. But now they're going to be incentivized to stay. And if that doesn't work, then we'll get even tougher than that. Okay?

We want our companies to hire and grow in America and to raise wages for American workers, and to help rebuild American cities and towns. (Applause.)

That is how we will all succeed together and grow together as one team, one people, and one American family. We want it to happen here. (Applause.)

Tax reform has not historically been a partisan issue, and it does not have to be a partisan issue today. I really believe we're going to have numerous Democrats come over and sign because it's the right thing to do. I believe that it's the right thing to do, and I know many of them. And they're telling me it is the right thing to do. President Reagan's tax cuts were passed with significant bipartisan majorities at a time when there was a Democrat majority in the House and a Democrat Speaker — Tip O'Neill.

Before that, Democrat President John F. Kennedy championed tax cuts that surged the economy and massively reduced unemployment. As President Kennedy very wisely said, "The single most important fiscal weapon available to strengthen the national economy is the federal tax policy. The right kind of tax cut at the right time" — at the right time, this is the right time — "is the most effective measure that this government could take to spur our economy forward." That was President Kennedy. (Applause.)

My fellow Americans, this is the right tax cut, and this is the right time. Democrats and Republicans in Congress should come together, finally, to deliver this giant win for the American people and begin middle-class miracle — it's called a middle-class miracle, once again. It's also called a miracle for our great companies; a miracle for the middle class, for the working person.

I truly believe that many Democrats want to support our plan, and with enough encouragement from the American people, they will find the courage to do what is right for our great country. (Applause.) But they'll only do it if you, the American people, make your voices heard. Only if you tell Congress to give us a tax code that puts American jobs first. And that's what we're doing. (Applause.)

History has proven time and time again that there is no power on Earth more awesome than the will of the American people. That is why today I am asking all Americans — Republican, Democrat, independent — to join with me, and with each other to demand tax reform that will truly, truly, truly make America great again. (Applause.)

Call your congressmen. Call your senators. Let them know you're watching. Let them know you're waiting. Tell them that today is the day for decision. That now is the time to heal this self-inflicted economic wound. And that with their action, the future will belong to all of us.

If you demand it, the politicians will listen. They will answer, and they will act. And someday, many years from now, our children and our grandchildren will remember this moment in history as the time when ordinary Americans took control of their destiny and chose a future of American patriotism, prosperity, and pride. (Applause.)

With your help and your voice, we will bring back our jobs, we will bring back our wealth, and for every citizen across this land, we will bring back our great American dreams.

Thank you, God bless you, and God bless the United States of America. (Applause.)

Remarks by President Trump on Tax Reform

President Trump discussed his plans to change the tax code in an August 30 speech in Springfield, Missouri.

THE PRESIDENT: Thank you very much. Thank you. (Applause.) Thank you very much. It's so nice. And we appreciate it. And all of the people outside that were waving proudly the American flag — believe me, we appreciate it very much.

I want to thank Jerry Cook, Steve Burney — (applause) — and all of the tremendous employees here at the Loren Cook Company for hosting us today. Where is Jerry? Where is Jerry? (Applause.) Thank you. Thank you, Jerry. What a job. I've heard so much about you. It's a great honor to know you, Jerry. Thank you.

I also want to welcome the many distinguished guests who are here with us for this very important event: Secretary of the Treasury, Steve Mnuchin. (Applause.) Thank you, Steve. Secretary of Commerce, Wilbur Ross. (Applause.) Small Business Administrator — which, by the way, is a very large business, I will tell you that — Linda McMahon, a friend of mine. (Applause.) And from the purely political world, a really great friend who did such an incredible job with his beautiful wife at the inauguration, Senator Roy Blunt. Thank you. Thank you. (Applause.) Where's Roy? Thank you, Roy.

Governor Greitens is here, who is doing some job. (Applause.) Thank you, Governor. Special. Lieutenant Governor Parson. Lieutenant Governor, thank you, Lieutenant Governor. And our great members of Commerce [Congress], I want to thank you all for coming. There are so many. I was asking the Governor and

Roy, I said, do you think I should announce them all? I have so many. But I'm honored that they're here.

Representative Sam Graves. (Applause.) Representative Vicky Hartzler, who has been terrific. (Applause.) My friend for a long time, and just somebody that he liked me from the beginning and I liked him, Billy Long. Where's Billy? (Applause.) Billy. Right, Billy? Right from the beginning. Blaine Luetkemeyer — where's Blaine? Good. Thank you, Blaine. (Applause.) Representative Jason Smith. (Applause.) Jason, thank you for everything, Jason. Representative Ann Wagner. Hi, Ann. Good job, Ann. (Applause.)

And, I don't know, we have so many more. Anybody I forgot? Right? Everything okay? Good, I got it. You, I remember more than anybody. Thank you all very much. I appreciate it. And to the congressmen and congresswomen, we very much appreciate you all being here. Thank you very much. (Applause.)

Before we begin, I'd like to take a few moments to discuss the deeply tragic situation in Texas and Louisiana. As we all know, our Gulf Coast was hit over the weekend with a devastating hurricane of historic proportion. Torrential rains and terrible flooding continue to pose a grave danger to life and to property. Our first responders have been doing absolutely heroic work to shepherd people out of harm's way, and their courage and devotion has saved countless lives. They represent truly the very best of America. (Applause.)

We must be vigilant. We must protect the lives of our people. I was on the ground in Texas yesterday to meet with Governor Abbott — who is doing, by the way, and incredible job — and local officials so that we could coordinate the very big and unprecedented federal response.

In difficult times such as these, we see the true character of the American people: their strength, their love, and their resolve. We see friend helping friend, neighbor helping neighbor, and stranger helping stranger. And together, we will endure and we will overcome. (Applause.)

To those affected by this storm, we are praying for you and we are here with you every single step of the way. And I can speak, I know, for the people in this room — every step of the way. (Applause.)

To those Americans who have lost loved ones: All of America is grieving with you, and our hearts are joined with yours forever. The citizens of Texas and the Gulf Coast need all the prayers, support, and resources our communities have to offer. Recovery will be tough, but I have seen the resilience of the American spirit firsthand, all over this country.

To the people of Houston, and across Texas and Louisiana: We are here with you today, we are with you tomorrow, and we will be with you every single day after to restore, recover, and rebuild.

As our thoughts and prayers remain firmly with the citizens and our fellow people — people — great, great people — all affected by this tragedy. We're also glad to be back in the heartland with the very, very fine folks of Missouri. (Applause.)

And I said to Senator Blunt and I said to Billy Long on the plane coming in — can I say "Missouri," or should I say "Missouruh"? Okay? And they said, whatever you want is okay. So I said, good. But I'm especially pleased to be here in Springfield, the birthplace of a great American icon, the legendary Route 66. Who would have known that? (Applause.)

This is the place where the "Main Street of America" got its start, and this is where America's main street will begin its big, beautiful comeback that — you are seeing it right now. This is a comeback of historic proportions. You're seeing it happen right now. (Applause.) Right? You're seeing it.

We're here today to launch our plans to bring back Main Street by reducing the crushing tax burden on our companies and on our workers. (Applause.) Our self-destructive tax code costs Americans millions and millions of jobs, trillions of dollars, and billions of hours spent on compliance and paperwork. And you have seen what's happening with regulations — they're going fast. We need regulations, but many of them are unnecessary, and they're going fast. (Applause.)

That is why the foundation of our job creation agenda is to fundamentally reform our tax code for the first time in more than 30 years. I want to work with Congress, Republicans and Democrats alike, on a plan that is pro-growth, pro-jobs, pro-worker — and pro-American. (Applause.)

There is no more fitting place to launch this effort than right here in the American heartland, surrounded by hardworking men and women whose skill, determination, and drive are truly second to none. (Applause.)

And, by the way, before I start, Ivanka Trump — I see my beautiful daughter is in the audience. Stand up, honey. (Applause.) She's working very hard. I'm very proud of Ivanka.

For many decades, Route 66 captured the American spirit. The communities along this historic route were a vivid symbol of America's booming industry. Truck drivers hauled made-in-America goods along this vital artery of commerce. Families passed through bustling towns on their way to explore the great American West. And high-quality manufacturing jobs lifted up communities, gave Americans a paycheck that could support a family. Mr. Cook is a great example of the people that do it. (Applause.) Stand up. Stand up Mr. Cook. Stand up. (Applause.) I think they like you. And provided millions of our fellow citizens with the pride and dignity that comes with work.

But, in recent years, millions of Americans have watched that prosperity slip away in the rearview mirror. And it wasn't pleasant to watch, especially for me. I would sit back — I was in business — and I could see what was happening. It wasn't good.

If we want to renew our prosperity, and to restore opportunity, then we must reduce the tax burden on our companies and on our workers. (Applause.)

In the last 10 years, our economy has grown at only around two percent a year. If you look at other countries and you look at what their GDP is, they're unhappy when it's seven, eight, nine. And I speak to them — leaders of the countries — how are you doing? "Not well, not well." Why? "GDP is down to seven percent." And I'm saying, we were hitting one percent just a number of months ago. So we're going to change that around, folks, that I can tell you. And we're going change it around fast. (Applause.)

And today — a very appropriate day that this should happen — we just announced that we hit three percent in GDP. It just came out. (Applause.) And on a yearly basis, as you know, the last administration, during an eight-year period, never hit three percent. So we're really on our way.

If we achieve sustained three percent growth, that means 12 million new jobs and $10 trillion dollars of new economic activity over the next decade. That's some numbers. (Applause.) And I happen to be one that thinks we can go much higher than three percent. There's no reason why we shouldn't. (Applause.)

So this is our once-in-a-generation opportunity to deliver real tax reform for everyday hardworking Americans, and I am fully committed to working with Congress to get this job done. And I don't want to be disappointed by Congress, do you understand me? Do you understand? (Applause.)

Congress — I think Congress is going to make a comeback. I hope so. (Laughter.) I tell you what, the United States is counting on it. (Applause.)

Here are my four principles for tax reform: First, we need a tax code that is simple, fair, and easy to understand. (Applause.) That means getting rid of the loopholes and complexity that primarily benefit the wealthiest Americans and special interests.

Our last major tax rewrite was 31 years ago. It eliminated dozens of loopholes and special interest tax breaks, reduced the number of tax brackets from fifteen to two, and lowered tax rates for both individuals and businesses. At the time, it was really something special.

Since then, our tax laws have tripled in size, and the tax code itself now spans more than 2,600 pages, and most of it is not understandable. Tax rates have increased, and special interest loopholes have crept back into the system. The tax code is now a massive source of complexity and frustration for tens of millions of Americans.

In 1935, the basic 1040 form that most people file had two simple pages of instructions. Today, that basic form has one hundred pages of instructions, and it's pretty complex stuff. The tax code is so complicated that more than 90 percent of Americans need professional help to do their own taxes.

This enormous complexity is very unfair. It disadvantages ordinary Americans who don't have an army of accountants while benefitting deep-pocketed special interests. And most importantly, this is wrong. (Applause.) Thank you.

First and foremost, our tax system should benefit loyal, hardworking Americans and their families. (Applause.) That is why tax reform must dramatically simplify the tax code, eliminate special interest loopholes — and I'm speaking against myself when I do this, I have to tell you. And I might be speaking against Mr. Cook, and we're both okay with it, is that right? It's crazy. We're speaking — maybe we shouldn't be doing this, you know? (Laughter.) But we're doing the right thing. (Applause.) True. And allow the vast majority of our citizens to file their taxes on a single, simple page without having to hire an accountant.

Second, we need a competitive tax code that creates more jobs and higher wages for Americans. It's time to give American workers the pay raise that they've been looking for for many, many years. (Applause.)

In 1986, Ronald Reagan led the world by cutting our corporate tax rate to 34 percent. That was below the average rate for developed countries at the time. Everybody thought that was a monumental thing that happened. But then, under this pro-America system, our economy boomed. It just went beautifully — right through the roof. The middle class thrived and median family income increased.

Other countries saw the success. They looked at us. They saw — what is America doing? What's happening with the United States? And they acted very swiftly by cutting their taxes lower, and lower, and lower, and reforming their tax systems to be far more competitive than ours.

Over the past 30 years, the average business tax rate among developed nations fell from 45 percent to less than 24 percent. And some countries have an unbelievably low tax, including, by the way, China and some others that are highly competitive, and really doing very well against us. They are taking us, frankly, to the cleaners. So we must — we have no choice — we must lower our taxes.

And your Senator, Claire McCaskill, she must do this for you. And if she doesn't do it for you, you have to have to vote her out of office. (Applause.) She's got to make that commitment. She's got to make that commitment. If she doesn't do it, you just can't do this anymore, with the obstruction and the obstructionists. If we don't get tax cuts and reform approved, potentially, the biggest ever — we are looking for the biggest ever — jobs and our country cannot take off the way they should, and it could be much worse than that. But, at a minimum, they won't take off the way they should.

The Dems are looking to obstruct tax cuts and tax reform, just like they obstructed so many other things, including administration appointments and healthcare. Not one vote. We got not one vote to try and fix healthcare and get rid of Obamacare.

The strategy of our economic rivals has worked. They made their taxes lower — and far lower, in many cases, than ours — and jobs left our country. Large corporations changed their business models by exporting jobs to other countries and then shipping their goods back to the United States, where they'd make massive profits, and they wouldn't be paying tax to us either. So we lost the jobs, we lost the taxes, they closed the buildings, they closed the plants and factories. We got nothing but unemployment. We got nothing.

Other businesses — even classic American brands — switched their headquarters to foreign countries. Because of this and other reasons, like weak borders, America remains stuck in the past. Although I have to tell you, we have General Kelly here today, and we stopped 78 percent — going up to 80 percent — on the border traffic coming through, in just a short period of time. (Applause.) He has done some job. A whole different world out there right now.

Today, we are still taxing our businesses at 35 percent, and it's way more than that. And think of it: In some cases, way above 40 percent when you include state and local taxes, in various states. The United States is now behind France, behind Germany, behind Canada, Ireland, Japan, Mexico, South Korea, and many other nations. Also, with these countries and almost every country, we have massive trade deficits — numbers that you would not believe.

But this administration is going to fix that. One by one, we're fixing it. We're working right now on NAFTA — the horrible, terrible NAFTA deal that took so much business out of your state and out of your cities and towns, and we're working on it. Let's see what happens. (Applause.)

Mexico is not happy. (Laughter.) But as I told them, you made a lot of money for a lot of years and everybody left you alone. We got to change this deal. And hopefully we can renegotiate it. But if we can't, we'll terminate it and we'll start all over again with a real deal. (Applause.)

So when it comes to the business tax, we are dead last. Can you believe that? So this cannot be allowed to continue any longer. America must lead the way, not follow from behind.

We have gone from a tax rate that is lower than our economic competitors, to one that is more than 60 percent higher. We have totally surrendered our competitive edge to other countries. We have totally surrendered. We're not surrendering anymore. (Applause.)

Ideally — and I say this for our Secretary of the Treasury — we would like to bring our business tax rate down to 15 percent, which would make our tax rate lower than most countries, but still, by no means the lowest, unfortunately, in the world. But it would make us highly competitive.

In other words, foreign companies have more than a 60 percent tax advantage over American companies. They can pay their workers more, sell their products and services at lower cost, and still make more money than their U.S. competitors.

We cannot restore our wealth if we continue to put our businesses at such a tremendous disadvantage. We must reduce the tax rate on American businesses so they keep jobs in America, create jobs in America, and compete for workers right here in America — the America we love. (Applause.) Thank you. Thank you very much.

Because when businesses compete for labor, your wages will go up. Lower taxes on American business means higher wages for American workers, and it means more products made right here in the USA. (Applause.)

When I was growing up, I always used to see the signs, and it was always stamped on the product: Made in the USA. You don't see it anymore. We're going to go back to Made in the USA — Made in the USA." (Applause.)

The third principle for tax reform is a crucial one: tax relief for middle-class families. (Applause.) In a way — and I've been saying this for a long time — they've been sort of the forgotten people, but they're not forgotten any longer. I can tell you that. (Applause.)

We will lower taxes for middle-income Americans so they can keep more of their hard-earned paychecks, and they can do lots of things with those paychecks. And that really means buying product ideally made in this country, but that means they'll go out, and they'll spend their money. And it will be a beautiful thing to watch. This includes helping parents afford childcare and the cost of raising a family. That's so important to Ivanka Trump. (Applause.) Very, very important to everybody in this room, but so important to my daughter. It's one of her real big beliefs. And she's very committed to that. Right, Ivanka?

We believe that ordinary Americans know better than Washington how to spend their own money, and we want to help them take home as much of their money as possible and then spend it. (Applause.) So they'll keep their money. They'll spend their money. They'll buy our product. Our factories will be moving again. Companies are going to move back into our country, jobs are going to prosper, and our country is going to be just like it says on that beautiful red hat — it says: Make America Great Again. That's what we're going to do. (Applause.) Right?

Fourth and finally, we want to bring back trillions of dollars in wealth that's parked overseas. Because of our high tax rate and horrible, outdated, bureaucratic rules, large companies that do business overseas will often park their profits offshore to avoid paying a high United States tax if the money is brought back home. So they leave the money over there.

The amount of money we're talking about is anywhere from $3 trillion to $5 trillion. Can you believe that? By making it less punitive for companies to bring back this money, and by making the process far less bureaucratic and difficult, we can return trillions and trillions of dollars to our economy and spur billions of dollars in new investments in our struggling communities and throughout our nation.

It's time to invest in our country, to rebuild our communities, and to hire our great American workers. (Applause.)

My administration is embracing a new economic model. It's called very simply: The American Model. Under this system, we will encourage companies to hire and grow in America, to raise wages for American workers, and to help rebuild our American cities and communities. That is how we will all succeed and grow together, as one team, with one shared sense of purpose, and one glorious American destiny. (Applause.)

So today I'm calling on all members of Congress — Democrat, Republican and independent — to support pro-American tax reform. They have to do it. It's time. (Applause.) They have to do it. It is time.

I'm calling on Congress to provide a level playing field for our workers and our companies, to attract new companies and businesses to our shores, and to put more money into the pockets of everyday, hardworking people and also into the pockets of our companies so they can continue to grow and expand. (Applause.)

What could possibly be more bipartisan than allowing families to keep more of what they earn and creating an environment for real job and wage growth in the country that we love so much? (Applause.)

So let's put — or at least try to put — the partisan posturing behind us and come together as Americans to create the 21st century tax code that our people deserve. (Applause.)

If we do this, if we unite in the name of common sense and the name of common good, then we will add millions and millions of new jobs, bring back trillions of dollars, and we will give America the competitive advantage that it so desperately needs and has been looking for for so long. It's time. (Applause.)

Products made with American hands, American labor, and American grit will once again be delivered throughout the world. It's true. (Applause.) It's time. Instead of exporting our jobs, we will export our goods. (Applause.) Our jobs will both stay here in America and come back to America. We'll have it both ways.

Millions of struggling citizens will be lifted from welfare to work. They will love getting up in the morning. They will love going to their job. They will love earning a big, fat, beautiful paycheck. They will be proud again. (Applause.)

That is the future I want for our people. That is the future I want for America — a nation where we are proud, prosperous, united, and free.

Today, I am asking every citizen to join me in dreaming big and bold and daring things — beautiful things — for our country. I am asking every member of Congress, of which we have many with us today, to join me in unleashing America's full potential. I am asking everyone in this room and across the nation to join me in demanding nothing but the best for our nation and for our people.

And if we do these things, and if we care for and support each other, and love each other, then we will truly make America great again.

Thank you. God bless you. (Applause.) God bless you, everybody. Thank you. Thank you very much. Governor, thank you. Thank you, Governor. Thank you, Senator. Thank you. Thank you, everybody.

Remarks by Trump on Infrastructure, Charlottesville

President Trump spoke at Trump Tower on Aug. 15, 2017, to discuss his plans to improve the nation's infrastructure. He also took questions from reporters about the alt-right rally in Charlottesville, Virginia.

THE PRESIDENT: Hello, everybody. Great to be back in New York with all of our friends, and some great friends outside the building, I must tell you. I want to thank all of our distinguished guests who are with us today, including members of our Cabinet: Treasury Secretary Steven Mnuchin, OMB Director Mick Mulvaney and, of course, our Transportation Secretary — who is doing a fabulous job — Elaine Chao.

Thank you all for doing a really incredible and creative job on what we're going to be discussing today, which is infrastructure. We've just had a great set of briefings upstairs on our infrastructure agenda. My administration is working every day to deliver the world-class infrastructure that our people deserve and, frankly, that our country deserves.

That's why I just signed a new executive order to dramatically reform the nation's badly broken infrastructure permitting process.

Just blocks away is the Empire State Building. It took 11 months to build the Empire State Building. But today, it can take as long as a decade and much more than that — many, many stories where it takes 20 and 25 years just to get approvals to start construction of a fairly routine highway. Highway builders must get up to 16 different approvals involving nine different federal agencies governed by 29 different statutes. One agency alone can stall a project for many, many years, and even decades.

Not only does this cost our economy billions of dollars, but it also denies our citizens the safe and modern infrastructure they deserve. This overregulated permitting process is a massive self-inflicted wound on our country — it's disgraceful — denying our people much-needed investments in their community.

And I just want to show you this because it was just shown to me, and I said, I think I'm going to show it to the media — both real and fake media, by the way. This is what it takes to get something approved today. Elaine, you see that? So this is what it takes. Permitting process flowchart — that's a flowchart.

So that can go out to 20 years. This shows about 10, but that can go out to about 20 years to get something approved. This is for a highway. I've seen a highway recently in a certain state — I won't mention its name — 17 years. I could have built it for four or five million dollars without the permitting process. It cost hundreds of millions of dollars, but it took 17 years to get it approved and many, many, many, many pages of environmental impact studies.

This is what we will bring it down to. This is less than two years. This is going to happen quickly. That's what I'm signing today. This will be less than two years for a highway. So it's going to be quick, it's going to be a very streamlined process. And, by the way, if it doesn't meet environmental safeguards, we're not going to approve it. Very simple. We're not going to approve it. Maybe this one will say, let's throw the other one away. Would anybody like it from the media? (Laughter.) Would anybody like that long, beautiful chart? You can have it.

So my executive order also requires agencies to work together efficiently by requiring one lead agency for each major infrastructure project. It also holds agencies accountable if they fail to streamline their review process. So each agency is accountable. We're going to get infrastructure built quickly, inexpensively — relatively speaking — and the permitting process will go very, very quickly.

No longer will we tolerate one job-killing delay after another. No longer will we accept a broken system that benefits consultants and lobbyists at the expense of hardworking Americans.

Now, I knew the process very well — probably better than anybody. I had to get permits for this building and many of the buildings I built — all of the buildings I built in Manhattan and many other places. And I will tell you that the consultants are rich people. They go around making it very difficult. They lobby Congress, they lobby state governments, city governments to make it very difficult so that you have to hire consultants, and that you have to take years and pay them a fortune. So we're streamlining the process, and we won't be having so much of that anymore.

No longer will we allow the infrastructure of our magnificent country to crumble and decay. While protecting the environment, we will build gleaming new roads, bridges, railways, waterways, tunnels, and highways. We will rebuild our country with American workers, American iron, American aluminum, American steel. We will create millions of new jobs and make millions of American dreams come true.

Our infrastructure will again be the best in the world. We used to have the greatest infrastructure anywhere in the world, and today we're like a third-world country. We are literally like a third-world country. Our infrastructure will again be the best, and we will restore the pride in our communities, our nation, and all over the United States we'll be proud again.

So I want to thank everybody for being here. God bless you. God bless the United States.

And if you have any questions, we have — Mick, you can come up here please. Come on up. Mick Mulvaney.

If you have any questions, please feel free to ask.

Q   Mr. President, why do you think these CEOs are leaving your manufacturing council?

THE PRESIDENT: Because they're not taking their job seriously as it pertains to this country. And we want jobs, manufacturing in this country. If you look at some of those people that you're talking about they're outside of the country, they're having a lot of their product made outsider. If you look at Merck as an example, take a look where — excuse me, excuse me — take a look at where their product is made. It's made outside of our country. We want products made in the country.

Now, I have to tell you, some of the folks that will leave, they're leaving out of embarrassment because they make their products outside. And I've been lecturing them, including the gentleman that you're referring to, about you have to bring it back to this country. You can't do it necessarily in Ireland and all of these other places. You have to bring this work back to this country. That's what I want. I want manufacturing to be back into the United States so that American workers can benefit.

Q   Let me ask you, Mr. President, why did you wait so long to blast neo-Nazis?

THE PRESIDENT: I didn't wait long.

Q   You waited two days —

THE PRESIDENT: I didn't wait long.

Q   Forty-eight hours.

THE PRESIDENT: I wanted to make sure, unlike most politicians, that what I said was correct — not make a quick statement. The statement I made on Saturday, the first statement, was a fine statement. But you don't make statements that direct unless you know the facts. It takes a little while to get the facts. You still don't know the facts. And it's a very, very important process to me, and it's a very important statement.

So I don't want to go quickly and just make a statement for the sake of making a political statement. I want to know the facts. If you go back to —

Q   So you had to (inaudible) white supremacists?

THE PRESIDENT: I brought it. I brought it. I brought it.

Q   Was it terrorism, in your opinion, what happened?

THE PRESIDENT: As I said on — remember, Saturday — we condemn in the strongest possible terms this egregious display of hatred, bigotry, and violence. It has no place in America. And then it went on from there.

Now, here's the thing —

Q   (Inaudible) many sides.

THE PRESIDENT: Excuse me. Excuse me. Take it nice and easy. Here's the thing: When I make a statement, I like to be correct. I want the facts. This event just happened. In fact, a lot of the event didn't even happen yet, as we were speaking. This event just happened.

Before I make a statement, I need the facts. So I don't want to rush into a statement. So making the statement when I made it was excellent. In fact, the young woman, who I hear was a fantastic young woman, and it was on NBC — her mother wrote me and said through, I guess, Twitter, social media, the nicest things. And I very much appreciated that. I hear she was a fine — really, actually, an incredible young woman. But her mother, on Twitter, thanked me for what I said.

And honestly, if the press were not fake, and if it was honest, the press would have said what I said was very nice. But unlike you, and unlike — excuse me, unlike you and unlike the media, before I make a statement, I like to know the facts.

Q   Why do Nazis like you — (inaudible) — these statements?

THE PRESIDENT: They don't. They don't.

Q   They do. Look —

(Cross-talk.)

THE PRESIDENT: How about a couple of infrastructure questions.

Q   Was it terrorism, that event? Was that terrorism?

Q   The CEO of Walmart said you missed a critical opportunity —

THE PRESIDENT: Say it. What?

Q   The CEO of Walmart said you missed a critical opportunity to help bring the country together. Did you?

THE PRESIDENT: Not at all. I think the country — look, you take a look. I've created over a million jobs since I'm President. The country is booming. The stock market is setting records. We have the highest employment numbers we've ever had in the history of our country. We're doing record business. We have the highest levels of enthusiasm. So the head of Walmart, who I know — who's a very nice guy — was making a political statement. I mean —

Q   (Inaudible.)

THE PRESIDENT: I'd do it the same way. And you know why? Because I want to make sure, when I make a statement, that the statement is correct. And there was no way — there was no way of making a correct statement that early. I had to see the facts, unlike a lot of reporters. Unlike a lot of reporters —

Q   Nazis were there.

Q   David Duke was there.

THE PRESIDENT: I didn't know David Duke was there. I wanted to see the facts. And the facts, as they started coming out, were very well stated. In fact, everybody said, "His statement was beautiful. If he would have made it sooner, that would have been good." I couldn't have made it sooner because I didn't know all of the facts. Frankly, people still don't know all of the facts.

It was very important — excuse me, excuse me — it was very important to me to get the facts out and correctly. Because if I would have made a fast statement — and the first statement was made without knowing much, other than what we were seeing. The second statement was made after, with knowledge, with great knowledge. There are still things — excuse me — there are still things that people don't know.

I want to make a statement with knowledge. I wanted to know the facts.

Q   Two questions. Was this terrorism? And can you tell us how you're feeling about your chief strategist, Stephen Bannon?

THE PRESIDENT: Well, I think the driver of the car is a disgrace to himself, his family, and this country. And that is — you can call it terrorism. You can call it murder. You can call it whatever you want. I would just call it as "the fastest one to come up with a good verdict." That's what I'd call it. Because there is a question: Is it murder? Is it terrorism? And then you get into legal semantics. The driver of the car is a murderer. And what he did was a horrible, horrible, inexcusable thing.

Q   Can you tell us how you're feeling about your chief strategist, Mr. Bannon? Can you talk about that?

THE PRESIDENT: Go ahead.

Q   I would echo Maggie's question. Steve Bannon has come under —

THE PRESIDENT: I never spoke to Mr. Bannon about it.

Q   Can you tell us broadly what your — do you still have confidence in Steve?

THE PRESIDENT: Well, we'll see. Look, look — I like Mr. Bannon. He's a friend of mine. But Mr. Bannon came on very late. You know that. I went through 17 senators, governors, and I won all the primaries. Mr. Bannon came on very much later than that. And I like him, he's a good man. He is not a racist, I can tell you that. He's a good person. He actually gets very unfair press in that regard. But we'll see what happens with Mr. Bannon. But he's a good person, and I think the press treats him, frankly, very unfairly.

Q   Senator McCain has called on you to defend your National Security Advisor, H.R. McMaster, against these attacks.

THE PRESIDENT: I did it the last time.

Q   And he called on it again, linking —

THE PRESIDENT: Senator McCain?

Q   — to the alt-right, and saying —

THE PRESIDENT: Senator McCain?

Q   Yes.

THE PRESIDENT: You mean the one who voted against Obamacare?

Q   And he said —

THE PRESIDENT: Who is — you mean Senator McCain who voted against us getting good healthcare?

Q   Senator McCain said that the alt-right is behind these attacks, and he linked that same group to those who perpetrated the attack in Charlottesville.

THE PRESIDENT: Well, I don't know. I can't tell you. I'm sure Senator McCain must know what he's talking about. But when you say the alt-right, define alt-right to me. You define it. Go ahead.

Q   Well, I'm saying, as Senator —

THE PRESIDENT: No, define it for me. Come on, let's go. Define it for me.

Q   Senator McCain defined them as the same group —

THE PRESIDENT: Okay, what about the alt-left that came charging at — excuse me, what about the alt-left that came charging at the, as you say, the alt-right? Do they have any semblance of guilt?

Let me ask you this: What about the fact that they came charging with clubs in their hands, swinging clubs? Do they have any problem? I think they do. As far as I'm concerned, that was a horrible, horrible day.

Q   You're not putting these —

THE PRESIDENT: Wait a minute. I'm not finished. I'm not finished, fake news. That was a horrible day —

Q   Sir, you're not putting these protestors on the same level as neo-Nazis —

Q   Is the alt-left as bad as white supremacy?

THE PRESIDENT: I will tell you something. I watched those very closely — much more closely than you people watched it. And you have — you had a group on one side that was bad, and

you had a group on the other side that was also very violent. And
nobody wants to say that, but I'll say it right now. You had a
group — you had a group on the other side that came charging in,
without a permit, and they were very, very violent.

Q   Is the alt-left as bad as Nazis? Are they as bad as Nazis?

THE PRESIDENT: Go ahead.

Q   Do you think that what you call the alt-left is the same as neo-
Nazis?

THE PRESIDENT: Those people — all of those people –excuse
me, I've condemned neo-Nazis. I've condemned many different
groups. But not all of those people were neo-Nazis, believe me.
 Not all of those people were white supremacists by any stretch.
 Those people were also there because they wanted to protest the
taking down of a statue of Robert E. Lee.

Q   Should that statue be taken down?

THE PRESIDENT: Excuse me. If you take a look at some of the
groups, and you see — and you'd know it if you were honest
reporters, which in many cases you're not — but many of those
people were there to protest the taking down of the statue of Robert
E. Lee.

So this week it's Robert E. Lee. I noticed that Stonewall Jackson
is coming down. I wonder, is it George Washington next week?
 And is it Thomas Jefferson the week after? You know, you really
do have to ask yourself, where does it stop?

But they were there to protest — excuse me, if you take a look, the
night before they were there to protest the taking down of the
statue of Robert E. Lee.

Infrastructure question. Go ahead.

Q   Should the statues of Robert E. Lee stay up?

THE PRESIDENT: I would say that's up to a local town, community, or the federal government, depending on where it is located.

Q   How concerned are you about race relations in America? And do you think things have gotten worse or better since you took office?

THE PRESIDENT: I think they've gotten better or the same. Look, they've been frayed for a long time. And you can ask President Obama about that, because he'd make speeches about it. But I believe that the fact that I brought in — it will be soon — millions of jobs — you see where companies are moving back into our country — I think that's going to have a tremendous, positive impact on race relations.

We have companies coming back into our country. We have two car companies that just announced. We have Foxconn in Wisconsin just announced. We have many companies, I say, pouring back into the country. I think that's going to have a huge, positive impact on race relations. You know why? It's jobs. What people want now, they want jobs. They want great jobs with good pay, and when they have that, you watch how race relations will be.

And I'll tell you, we're spending a lot of money on the inner cities. We're fixing the inner cities. We're doing far more than anybody has done with respect to the inner cities. It's a priority for me, and it's very important.

Q   Mr. President, are you putting what you're calling the alt-left and white supremacists on the same moral plane?

THE PRESIDENT: I'm not putting anybody on a moral plane. What I'm saying is this: You had a group on one side and you had a group on the other, and they came at each other with clubs — and it was vicious and it was horrible. And it was a horrible thing to watch.

But there is another side. There was a group on this side. You can call them the left — you just called them the left — that came violently attacking the other group. So you can say what you want, but that's the way it is.

Q   (Inaudible) both sides, sir. You said there was hatred, there was violence on both sides. Are the —

THE PRESIDENT: Yes, I think there's blame on both sides. If you look at both sides — I think there's blame on both sides. And I have no doubt about it, and you don't have any doubt about it either.

And if you reported it accurately, you would say.

Q   The neo-Nazis started this. They showed up in Charlottesville to protest —

THE PRESIDENT: Excuse me, excuse me. They didn't put themselves — and you had some very bad people in that group, but you also had people that were very fine people, on both sides. You had people in that group.

Q   (Inaudible.)

THE PRESIDENT: Excuse me, excuse me. I saw the same pictures as you did.

You had people in that group that were there to protest the taking down of, to them, a very, very important statue and the renaming of a park from Robert E. Lee to another name.

Q   George Washington and Robert E. Lee are not the same.

THE PRESIDENT: George Washington was a slave owner. Was George Washington a slave owner? So will George Washington now lose his status? Are we going to take down —

Excuse me, are we going to take down statues to George Washington? How about Thomas Jefferson? What do you think of Thomas Jefferson? You like him?

Q   I do love Thomas Jefferson.

THE PRESIDENT: Okay, good. Are we going to take down the statue? Because he was a major slave owner. Now, are we going to take down his statue?

So you know what, it's fine. You're changing history. You're changing culture. And you had people — and I'm not talking about the neo-Nazis and the white nationalists — because they should be condemned totally. But you had many people in that group other than neo-Nazis and white nationalists. Okay? And the press has treated them absolutely unfairly.

Now, in the other group also, you had some fine people. But you also had troublemakers, and you see them come with the black outfits and with the helmets, and with the baseball bats. You had a lot of bad people in the other group.

Q   Who are the good people?

Q   Sir, I just didn't understand what you were saying. You were saying the press has treated white nationalists unfairly? I just don't understand what you were saying.

THE PRESIDENT: No, no. There were people in that rally — and I looked the night before — if you look, there were people protesting very quietly the taking down of the statue of Robert E. Lee. I'm sure in that group there were some bad ones. The following day it looked like they had some rough, bad people — neo-Nazis, white nationalists, whatever you want to call them.

But you had a lot of people in that group that were there to innocently protest, and very legally protest — because I don't know if you know, they had a permit. The other group didn't have a permit. So I only tell you this: There are two sides to a story. I

thought what took place was a horrible moment for our country —
a horrible moment. But there are two sides to the country.

Does anybody have a final —

Q   I have an infrastructure question.

THE PRESIDENT: You have an infrastructure —

Q   What makes you think you can get an infrastructure bill? You
didn't get healthcare —

THE PRESIDENT: Well, you know, I'll tell you. We came very
close with healthcare. Unfortunately, John McCain decided to
vote against it at the last minute. You'll have to ask John McCain
why he did that. But we came very close to healthcare. We will
end up getting healthcare. But we'll get the infrastructure. And
actually, infrastructure is something that I think we'll have
bipartisan support on. I actually think Democrats will go along
with the infrastructure.

Q   Mr. President, have you spoken to the family of the victim of
the car attack?

THE PRESIDENT: No, I'll be reaching out. I'll be reaching out.

Q   When will you be reaching out?

THE PRESIDENT: I thought that the statement put out — the
mother's statement I thought was a beautiful statement. I will tell
you, it was something that I really appreciated. I thought it was
terrific. And, really, under the kind of stress that she's under and
the heartache that she's under, I thought putting out that statement,
to me, was really something. I won't forget it.

Thank you, all, very much. Thank you. Thank you.

* * * *

Q   Will you go to Charlottesville? Will you go to check out what happened?

THE PRESIDENT: I own a house in Charlottesville. Does anyone know I own a house in Charlottesville?

Q   Where is it?

THE PRESIDENT: Oh boy, it's going to be —

Q   Where is it?

THE PRESIDENT: It's in Charlottesville. You'll see.

Q   Is it a winery or something?

THE PRESIDENT: It is the winery.

I mean, I know a lot about Charlottesville. Charlottesville is a great place that's been very badly hurt over the last couple of days.

Q   (Inaudible.)

THE PRESIDENT: I own, actually, one of the largest wineries in the United States. It's in Charlottesville.

Q   Do you believe your words are helping to heal this country right now?

Q   What do you think needs to be done to overcome the racial divides in this country?

THE PRESIDENT: Well, I think jobs can have a big impact. I think if we continue to create jobs — over a million, substantially more than a million. And you see just the other day, the car companies coming in with Foxconn. I think if we continue to create jobs at levels that I'm creating jobs, I think that's going to have a tremendous impact — positive impact on race relations.

Q   Your remarks today, how do you think that will impact the racial, sort of conflict, today?

THE PRESIDENT: The people are going to be working, they're going to be making a lot of money — much more money than they ever thought possible. But that's going to happen.

Q   Your remarks today.

THE PRESIDENT: And the other thing — very important — I believe wages will start going up. They haven't gone up for a long time. I believe wages now — because the economy is doing so well with respect to employment and unemployment, I believe wages will start to go up. I think that will have a tremendously positive impact on race relations.

President Trump on the Paris Climate Accord

President Trump spoke in the Rose Garden on June 1, 2017, to announce that the United States would withdraw from the Paris Agreement, a global accord aimed at addressing climate change.

THE PRESIDENT: Thank you very much. (Applause.) Thank you. I would like to begin by addressing the terrorist attack in Manila. We're closely monitoring the situation, and I will continue to give updates if anything happens during this period of time. But it is really very sad as to what's going on throughout the world with terror. Our thoughts and our prayers are with all of those affected.

Before we discuss the Paris Accord, I'd like to begin with an update on our tremendous — absolutely tremendous — economic progress since Election Day on November 8th. The economy is starting to come back, and very, very rapidly. We've added $3.3 trillion in stock market value to our economy, and more than a million private sector jobs.

I have just returned from a trip overseas where we concluded nearly $350 billion of military and economic development for the United States, creating hundreds of thousands of jobs. It was a very, very successful trip, believe me. (Applause.) Thank you. Thank you.

In my meetings at the G7, we have taken historic steps to demand fair and reciprocal trade that gives Americans a level playing field against other nations. We're also working very hard for peace in the Middle East, and perhaps even peace between the Israelis and the Palestinians. Our attacks on terrorism are greatly stepped up

— and you see that, you see it all over — from the previous administration, including getting many other countries to make major contributions to the fight against terror. Big, big contributions are being made by countries that weren't doing so much in the form of contribution.

One by one, we are keeping the promises I made to the American people during my campaign for President –- whether it's cutting job-killing regulations; appointing and confirming a tremendous Supreme Court justice; putting in place tough new ethics rules; achieving a record reduction in illegal immigration on our southern border; or bringing jobs, plants, and factories back into the United States at numbers which no one until this point thought even possible. And believe me, we've just begun. The fruits of our labor will be seen very shortly even more so.

On these issues and so many more, we're following through on our commitments. And I don't want anything to get in our way. I am fighting every day for the great people of this country. Therefore, in order to fulfill my solemn duty to protect America and its citizens, the United States will withdraw from the Paris Climate Accord — (applause) — thank you, thank you — but begin negotiations to reenter either the Paris Accord or a really entirely new transaction on terms that are fair to the United States, its businesses, its workers, its people, its taxpayers. So we're getting out. But we will start to negotiate, and we will see if we can make a deal that's fair. And if we can, that's great. And if we can't, that's fine. (Applause.)

As President, I can put no other consideration before the wellbeing of American citizens. The Paris Climate Accord is simply the latest example of Washington entering into an agreement that disadvantages the United States to the exclusive benefit of other countries, leaving American workers — who I love — and taxpayers to absorb the cost in terms of lost jobs, lower wages, shuttered factories, and vastly diminished economic production.

Thus, as of today, the United States will cease all implementation of the non-binding Paris Accord and the draconian financial and economic burdens the agreement imposes on our country. This includes ending the implementation of the nationally determined contribution and, very importantly, the Green Climate Fund which is costing the United States a vast fortune.

Compliance with the terms of the Paris Accord and the onerous energy restrictions it has placed on the United States could cost America as much as 2.7 million lost jobs by 2025 according to the National Economic Research Associates. This includes 440,000 fewer manufacturing jobs — not what we need — believe me, this is not what we need — including automobile jobs, and the further decimation of vital American industries on which countless communities rely. They rely for so much, and we would be giving them so little.

According to this same study, by 2040, compliance with the commitments put into place by the previous administration would cut production for the following sectors: paper down 12 percent; cement down 23 percent; iron and steel down 38 percent; coal — and I happen to love the coal miners — down 86 percent; natural gas down 31 percent. The cost to the economy at this time would be close to $3 trillion in lost GDP and 6.5 million industrial jobs, while households would have $7,000 less income and, in many cases, much worse than that.

Not only does this deal subject our citizens to harsh economic restrictions, it fails to live up to our environmental ideals. As someone who cares deeply about the environment, which I do, I cannot in good conscience support a deal that punishes the United States — which is what it does -- the world's leader in environmental protection, while imposing no meaningful obligations on the world's leading polluters.

For example, under the agreement, China will be able to increase these emissions by a staggering number of years — 13. They can do whatever they want for 13 years. Not us. India makes its participation contingent on receiving billions and billions and billions of dollars in foreign aid from developed countries. There are many other examples. But the bottom line is that the Paris Accord is very unfair, at the highest level, to the United States.

Further, while the current agreement effectively blocks the development of clean coal in America — which it does, and the mines are starting to open up. We're having a big opening in two weeks. Pennsylvania, Ohio, West Virginia, so many places. A big opening of a brand-new mine. It's unheard of. For many, many years, that hasn't happened. They asked me if I'd go. I'm going to try.

China will be allowed to build hundreds of additional coal plants. So we can't build the plants, but they can, according to this agreement. India will be allowed to double its coal production by 2020. Think of it: India can double their coal production. We're supposed to get rid of ours. Even Europe is allowed to continue construction of coal plants.

In short, the agreement doesn't eliminate coal jobs, it just transfers those jobs out of America and the United States, and ships them to foreign countries.

This agreement is less about the climate and more about other countries gaining a financial advantage over the United States. The rest of the world applauded when we signed the Paris Agreement — they went wild; they were so happy — for the simple reason that it put our country, the United States of America, which we all love, at a very, very big economic disadvantage. A cynic would say the obvious reason for economic competitors and their wish to see us remain in the agreement is so that we continue to suffer this self-inflicted major economic wound. We would find it very hard to compete with other countries from other parts of the world.

We have among the most abundant energy reserves on the planet, sufficient to lift millions of America's poorest workers out of poverty. Yet, under this agreement, we are effectively putting these reserves under lock and key, taking away the great wealth of our nation — it's great wealth, it's phenomenal wealth; not so long ago, we had no idea we had such wealth — and leaving millions and millions of families trapped in poverty and joblessness.

The agreement is a massive redistribution of United States wealth to other countries. At 1 percent growth, renewable sources of energy can meet some of our domestic demand, but at 3 or 4 percent growth, which I expect, we need all forms of available American energy, or our country — (applause) — will be at grave risk of brownouts and blackouts, our businesses will come to a halt in many cases, and the American family will suffer the consequences in the form of lost jobs and a very diminished quality of life.

Even if the Paris Agreement were implemented in full, with total compliance from all nations, it is estimated it would only produce a two-tenths of one degree — think of that; this much — Celsius reduction in global temperature by the year 2100. Tiny, tiny amount. In fact, 14 days of carbon emissions from China alone would wipe out the gains from America — and this is an incredible statistic — would totally wipe out the gains from America's expected reductions in the year 2030, after we have had to spend billions and billions of dollars, lost jobs, closed factories, and suffered much higher energy costs for our businesses and for our homes.

As the Wall Street Journal wrote this morning: "The reality is that withdrawing is in America's economic interest and won't matter much to the climate." The United States, under the Trump administration, will continue to be the cleanest and most environmentally friendly country on Earth. We'll be the cleanest. We're going to have the cleanest air. We're going to have the cleanest water. We will be environmentally friendly, but we're not going to put our businesses out of work and we're not going to lose our jobs. We're going to grow; we're going to grow rapidly. (Applause.)

And I think you just read — it just came out minutes ago, the small business report — small businesses as of just now are booming, hiring people. One of the best reports they've seen in many years.

I'm willing to immediately work with Democratic leaders to either negotiate our way back into Paris, under the terms that are fair to the United States and its workers, or to negotiate a new deal that protects our country and its taxpayers. (Applause.)

So if the obstructionists want to get together with me, let's make them non-obstructionists. We will all sit down, and we will get back into the deal. And we'll make it good, and we won't be closing up our factories, and we won't be losing our jobs. And we'll sit down with the Democrats and all of the people that represent either the Paris Accord or something that we can do that's much better than the Paris Accord. And I think the people of our country will be thrilled, and I think then the people of the world will be thrilled. But until we do that, we're out of the agreement.

I will work to ensure that America remains the world's leader on environmental issues, but under a framework that is fair and where the burdens and responsibilities are equally shared among the many nations all around the world.

No responsible leader can put the workers — and the people — of their country at this debilitating and tremendous disadvantage. The fact that the Paris deal hamstrings the United States, while empowering some of the world's top polluting countries, should dispel any doubt as to the real reason why foreign lobbyists wish to keep our magnificent country tied up and bound down by this agreement: It's to give their country an economic edge over the United States. That's not going to happen while I'm President. I'm sorry. (Applause.)

My job as President is to do everything within my power to give America a level playing field and to create the economic, regulatory and tax structures that make America the most prosperous and productive country on Earth, and with the highest standard of living and the highest standard of environmental protection.

Our tax bill is moving along in Congress, and I believe it's doing very well. I think a lot of people will be very pleasantly surprised. The Republicans are working very, very hard. We'd love to have support from the Democrats, but we may have to go it alone. But it's going very well.

The Paris Agreement handicaps the United States economy in order to win praise from the very foreign capitals and global activists that have long sought to gain wealth at our country's expense. They don't put America first. I do, and I always will. (Applause.)

The same nations asking us to stay in the agreement are the countries that have collectively cost America trillions of dollars through tough trade practices and, in many cases, lax contributions to our critical military alliance. You see what's happening. It's pretty obvious to those that want to keep an open mind.

At what point does America get demeaned? At what point do they start laughing at us as a country? We want fair treatment for its citizens, and we want fair treatment for our taxpayers. We don't want other leaders and other countries laughing at us anymore. And they won't be. They won't be.

I was elected to represent the citizens of Pittsburgh, not Paris. (Applause.) I promised I would exit or renegotiate any deal which fails to serve America's interests. Many trade deals will soon be under renegotiation. Very rarely do we have a deal that works for this country, but they'll soon be under renegotiation. The process has begun from day one. But now we're down to business.

Beyond the severe energy restrictions inflicted by the Paris Accord, it includes yet another scheme to redistribute wealth out of the United States through the so-called Green Climate Fund — nice name — which calls for developed countries to send $100 billion to developing countries all on top of America's existing and massive foreign aid payments. So we're going to be paying billions and billions and billions of dollars, and we're already way ahead of anybody else. Many of the other countries haven't spent anything, and many of them will never pay one dime.

The Green Fund would likely obligate the United States to commit potentially tens of billions of dollars of which the United States has already handed over $1 billion — nobody else is even close; most of them haven't even paid anything — including funds raided out of America's budget for the war against terrorism. That's where they came. Believe me, they didn't come from me. They came just before I came into office. Not good. And not good the way they took the money.

In 2015, the United Nation's departing top climate officials reportedly described the $100 billion per year as "peanuts," and stated that "the $100 billion is the tail that wags the dog." In 2015, the Green Climate Fund's executive director reportedly stated that estimated funding needed would increase to $450 billion per year after 2020. And nobody even knows where the money is going to. Nobody has been able to say, where is it going to?

Of course, the world's top polluters have no affirmative obligations under the Green Fund, which we terminated. America is $20 trillion in debt. Cash-strapped cities cannot hire enough police officers or fix vital infrastructure. Millions of our citizens are out of work. And yet, under the Paris Accord, billions of dollars that ought to be invested right here in America will be sent to the very countries that have taken our factories and our jobs away from us. So think of that.

There are serious legal and constitutional issues as well. Foreign leaders in Europe, Asia, and across the world should not have more to say with respect to the U.S. economy than our own citizens and their elected representatives. Thus, our withdrawal from the agreement represents a reassertion of America's sovereignty. (Applause.) Our Constitution is unique among all the nations of the world, and it is my highest obligation and greatest honor to protect it. And I will.

Staying in the agreement could also pose serious obstacles for the United States as we begin the process of unlocking the restrictions on America's abundant energy reserves, which we have started very strongly. It would once have been unthinkable that an international agreement could prevent the United States from conducting its own domestic economic affairs, but this is the new reality we face if we do not leave the agreement or if we do not negotiate a far better deal.

The risks grow as historically these agreements only tend to become more and more ambitious over time. In other words, the Paris framework is a starting point — as bad as it is — not an end point. And exiting the agreement protects the United States from future intrusions on the United States' sovereignty and massive future legal liability. Believe me, we have massive legal liability if we stay in.

As President, I have one obligation, and that obligation is to the American people. The Paris Accord would undermine our economy, hamstring our workers, weaken our sovereignty, impose unacceptable legal risks, and put us at a permanent disadvantage to the other countries of the world. It is time to exit the Paris Accord — (applause) — and time to pursue a new deal that protects the environment, our companies, our citizens, and our country.

It is time to put Youngstown, Ohio, Detroit, Michigan, and Pittsburgh, Pennsylvania — along with many, many other locations within our great country — before Paris, France. It is time to make America great again. (Applause.) Thank you. Thank you. Thank you very much.

Thank you very much. Very important. I'd like to ask Scott Pruitt, who most of you know and respect, as I do, just to say a few words.

Remarks by the President at the NRCC Dinner

President Donald Trump spoke at a fundraiser for the National Republican Congressional Committee on March 21, 2017, in Washington, D.C.

THE PRESIDENT: Thank you very much. Thank you. Wow. You know, I asked how many people would be here tonight. They said a couple of hundred. It was just like a little fundraiser. They didn't say you broke — 23 years, you broke the all-time record tonight — $30.1 million. And broke it by $10 million — that's not so close. So, congratulations. We're going to have a great eight years together. (Applause.)

And Rasmussen just came out with a very good poll — you'll be liking this poll. This poll is good. We're going to do a good job. More importantly, we're going to do a great job, and then we're going to win it the old-fashioned way — we're just going to win it. And I want to thank everybody.

This is a lot more than 200 people. This is a hell of a big room. (Laughter.) That's far back. Can you see over there? See, I would have gotten rid of these columns, actually. (Laughter.) That's being a construction man. But that was a long time ago, they didn't do that.

Well, it's an honor to address you tonight, and thank each and every one of you for your role in helping to build, sustain and grow a truly strong Republican Party again.

In this effort, we will be working hand-in-hand with our House leadership team — and I've really gotten to know them and they are winners and they are terrific people — terrific people. (Applause.) Speaker Paul Ryan, Leader Kevin McCarthy, Majority Whip Steve Scalise, and Conference Chairwoman Cathy McMorris Rodgers. What a group, great group (Applause.)

Also with us tonight — a man who I have a lot respect for, gave me a very early endorsement — former Vice President Dick Cheney, along with his daughter, Congressman Liz Cheney. (Applause.) Where is he? Thank you, Dick. Thank you. Thank you, Liz.

I also want to thank the Chairman of the Republican Congressional — I mean, look, what a group — Committee. Where is Steve? Where is he? They lost him backstage. Steve Stivers — where is he? Steve, what the hell happened? I think he left. (Laughter.) Everyone is looking — it's the second time he's been introduced. Steve, are you there? Oh. Come here, Steve. What a job you did. Come here, Steve. He's embarrassed. (Laughter.) Come here, come on, get up here, Steve. Come here. (Applause.)

MR. STIVERS: Thanks, everybody.

THE PRESIDENT: That's what I like. See, that's a real worker. Oh, boy — no talk, all action, right? We like people like that. Congratulations to Steve.

And March Dinner Chairman, Steve Womack, and the NRCC Finance Chair, Ann Wagner — thank you. Thank you, Ann. (Applause.)

The work of the NRCC never ends. In fact, we have four special elections currently underway in Georgia — we won — Montana — we won — Kansas — we won — and South Carolina. We love South Carolina. That's some group. Where's South Carolina? Oh, we love South Carolina. Remember I was supposed to lose that one big and we won by 21 points. And that's when I found out these polls are rigged. (Laughter.) They were rigged. Thank you, South Carolina. I learned a lot from South Carolina.

Our nominees from Montana and Kansas are here with us this evening — Greg Gianforte and Ron Estes. Thank you. Thank you very much. (Applause.) Thank you.

On November 8th, the American People voted for historic change — and they also voted for serious action. By delivering the House, the Senate and the White House, the American people gave us clear instructions: It's time to get busy, get to work, and to get the job done. (Applause.)

That legislative effort begins with Thursday's crucial vote — and it really is a crucial vote for the Republican Party and for the people of our country — to finally repeal and replace the disaster known as Obamacare. It's what it is, a disaster. Premiums have soared double digits and even triple digits. Insurance companies are fleeing. One-third of counties only have one Obamacare insurer left. I was in Tennessee four nights ago — they've lost half the state. The insurance companies are gone and they're going to lose the next one pretty soon from what they say. And last night in Kentucky, we had a tremendous crowd — 25,000 people, more — and a similar crowd in Tennessee, by the way — packed, with thousands of people outside. They couldn't get them into these massive arenas — there's something going on that's really incredible in this country. It's really incredible.

But Kentucky also is having a tremendous problem, as you know and as you've read, with Obamacare. And many other states. The House bill ends the Obamacare nightmare and gives healthcare decisions back to the states — and back to the American people.

These are the conservative solutions we campaigned on, and these are the conservative solutions the American people asked us as a group to deliver. We are keeping our promises. I go to these arenas, and they have signs all over the place — He's kept his promise. He's kept his promise. Because I've done a lot of work.

The border is in the best shape it's been in in decades. Down 61 percent since inauguration. (Applause.) General Kelly — you know, they used to put political people — I refuse to say political hacks because I would not say that. Because there is no such thing as a political hack. But they would put nice political people at the border. I put General Kelly — recommended by General "Mad Dog" Mattis. (Applause.)

I said to him, General — General Mattis — I said, General, I need somebody really smart and really tough for the border. Sir, I have the man — General Kelly. Soon as I saw him it was like — an interview lasted for about 30 seconds — I said, he's the right guy. And he's been great. And General Mattis has been great — you see what's going on. Big difference.

It's been 60 days since my inauguration, and that was a promise that I've really kept.

As you saw today in the Senate, I nominated a Supreme Court justice who will uphold and defend the Constitution of the United States. (Applause.)

I've taken historic action to eliminate unnecessary, job-killing regulations. And we've just started on that one. (Applause.) But we've gotten rid of a lot of them. That includes eliminating regulations crushing our coal industry. We're going to put our great coal miners back to work. Clean coal. Clean coal. (Applause.)

I've cleared the way for the Dakota Access and Keystone XL pipelines — and added a requirement that American pipelines be constructed with American steel. That was the last minute. I said, where are we getting the steel? I won't tell you where, but you can guess. I said, from now on we have to go — we have to build them here. You want to put pipelines under our land you're going to make the pipe in this country. (Applause.)

And one other thing happened. I have to tell you, it's sort of interesting. So I get a call from the ex-president of Goldman Sachs who now works for — Gary Cohn. I said to him, Gary, let me ask you — I heard there was a lawsuit. I hear the pipeline company is suing us. I said, how much? $14 billion. I said, wait a minute.

 I'm approving the pipeline and they're suing us for $14 billion, and I've already approved it, right? I said, I just heard it. Go back to them and tell them if they don't drop the suit immediately we are going to terminate the deal You have great — you know, being President gives you great power, right? (Laughter.) So I just saw him this morning — I said, by the way, how did you do? He said, sir, they dropped the suit. Good. (Applause.)

Isn't that easier — look, if I'm — do you think Hillary does that? I don't think so. I don't think so. Isn't that easier, though, than settling for like $4 billion seven years from now? Oh, but the lawyers aren't happy at all. They don't like it. You got a lot of lawyers in this crowd — they're not happy about that deal.

Because of the new business climate that we're creating, jobs are already starting to pour back in — companies like Sprint, Intel, Exxon-Mobile — where a great man, Rex Tillerson, is doing an incredible job — (applause) — ran that company for many years and ran it well. Walmart, Ford, Fiat-Chrysler and General Motors have all announced that they're keeping or adding tens of thousands of jobs right here in America. A big difference. We used to hear they're all leaving. Now they're all coming back. They're coming back, too, believe me. If they don't, we're taxing the hell out of their products, so you know they're coming back. (Applause.)

Why didn't somebody start doing that 25 years ago? One company said, sir, we're building a big plant — there's nothing we can do to stop it. It's already under construction. I said, here's the story — when you make your cars, or whatever, and you fire all our American employees, and then you think in your new plant — beautiful new plant, congratulations — you're going to sell that product our border, tax-free, you're wrong — 35 percent tax. It's amazing how quickly they say, you know, I think we've decided to stay in the United States.

I only wonder, why didn't somebody do this like 25 years ago? You would have had nobody leaving. So far, I think I'm batting about 100 percent.

To save taxpayer dollars, I've already begun negotiating better contracts for the federal government — saving over $700 million on just one set of airplanes of which there are many sets.

As I promised during the campaign, I have proposed a budget that eliminates the defense sequester and fully rebuilds the United States military. We need it more than ever. (Applause.) We need it more than ever. We've got a lot of haters out there — they hate. We got some people running some countries that are bad people. We will take care of it. We will ensure that the America warrior — and if you think about it, the great American warriors — because that's what they are — are given the tools, the funding, the resources, the training and equipment they so richly deserve. They are warriors, and they have old equipment. They're not going to have old equipment much longer.

And we will take care of our great veterans. What's happening there is going to be incredible. Finally, we're going to take care of our veterans. (Applause.) Our defense expansion will fully pay — and this will be something that is so important — it will be fully paid by making government leaner, more accountable and just perfect for our people. But I will tell you, if it's not fully paid — because we're doing a big number, with the planes and the ships — our Navy is at World War I levels. Can you believe that? World War I levels. So if we don't fully pay, we're going to do a little work, but we're going to get our military rebuilt — bigger and better and stronger than ever — because we have no choice, folks. There's some bad players out there. (Applause.) And it's going to go quickly.

I have also followed through on my promise to secure, protect and defend the borders of the United States — and, yes, we will build a great border wall at our Southern border. (Applause.) It will be built. These security actions will save billions of dollars, millions of jobs, and thousands and thousands of lives. We're also taking decisive action to improve our vetting procedures. The courts are not helping us, I have to be honest with you. Ridiculous. Somebody said I should not criticize judges. Okay, I'll criticize judges. (Laughter.) To keep criminals and terrorists the hell out of our country.

We are keeping these promises, and many, many more. After we repeal and replace Obamacare, our Republican majority will pass massive, historic tax reform — the biggest tax cut since Ronald Reagan, and potentially even bigger. It's going to be very big. (Applause.) And by the way, we had to go — had no choice — had to go with the healthcare first. You know how it works. This is one room that really does know how it works. But we had to go with the healthcare first. And we're doing well. I think we're going to have some great surprises. I hope that it's going to all work out.

Then we immediately start on the tax cuts, and they're going to be really fantastic, and I am looking forward to that one. That one is going to be fun. That one is going to be fun. That's called the wheelhouse. We're going to do a great job for companies. We're going to bring back — could be $3 to $5 trillion from overseas, money that can't be brought back as part of our taxes. (Applause.)

And it will lower the business tax rate from one of the highest in the world to one of the most competitive anywhere in the world. Way, way down. (Applause.) We will do everything we can to lower business burdens and to make it easier for our businesses to thrive and compete. But in exchange, they must hire, invest and grow in America. We're not giving them anything — okay? They got to do that. That's the one thing.

We're working with the automobile industry who have been played around with. And I'm saying, we'll do things for you, but you got to build new plants all over the place. You got to build new plants in our country. And they're doing it, they're starting. It's going to be amazing.

I have called this model, the model that you've been watching, the model that's created so much value, the model of bringing back jobs and bringing back industry — I called it the American Model. And this is the system that our Founders wanted. Our greatest

American leaders — including George Washington, Hamilton, Jackson, Lincoln — they all agreed that for America to be a strong nation it must also be a great manufacturing nation. Have to make money.

The Republican platform of 1896 — more than a century ago — stated that: "Protection and reciprocity are twin measures of American policy and go hand in hand." I mean, we have situations where other countries who have zero respect for our country — by the way, do you notice they're starting to respect us a lot? A lot. A lot. They'll charge us 100 percent tax on some — 100 percent. And we charge them nothing. They'll make it impossible through regulations for our product to be sold in their country, and yet they'll sell their product routinely in our country. Not going to happen anymore. The word, "reciprocity" — they do it, we do it. Who can complain about that? Big difference. You're talking about big, big dollars, too, by the way.

The platform went on to say: "We renew and emphasize our allegiance to the policy of protection, as the bulwark of American industrial independence and the foundation of American development and prosperity."

Now, these were some of our greatest leaders, some of whom were great businesspeople. They understood we have to do it. And just so you understand, I'm a free trader, but free trade has been very unfair trade. So I now say I'm a fair trader. And I want to trade all over the world. I don't want to have it just here. But we're going to be beneficiaries from now on. We're not going to be the people that are taken advantage of any longer. That's been happening for decades and decades — not going to happen any longer. (Applause.) And they know it.

One country came in to see me recently — big country, good country, great person. One of his first questions, sir, how much will you be charging us? It's like he knew. He knew. (Laughter.) He knew. They've been ripping us for years and he finally saw somebody that understands — so it's one of those — (laughter.) You don't mind having a rich nation again and having lower taxes, do you? Does anybody here mind? Anybody mind, please stand up. I know Dick Cheney will not stand on this one. Please stand up.

As long as the GOP stands for "Made in the USA," — remember in the old days, cars all said, "Made in the USA," right? We don't have that too much anymore. We're going to have it again soon. I'm telling all the car companies, put a big label, "Made in the USA" — it's going to stand for quality.   Our party will have a very, very bright future.

It is fitting that we are in the National Building Museum. Since its founding, the Republican Party has been a party of builders. Many of the great builders are in this audience tonight. Some of them I have to compete with and I really — actually, I don't like very many of them. (Laughter.) Some of them I do. Some of them I truly dislike a lot. (Laughter.)

But now I like everybody. I like all the great builders. See, now it's different. (Laughter.) Now we're all on the same side, so I like — see the guy over there? I couldn't stand that guy for years. He did a good job, but I couldn't stand him. Now I like you. (Laughter.)

Our first Republican President, Abraham Lincoln, ran his first campaign for public office in 1832 — when he was only 23 years old. He began by imagining the benefits a railroad could bring to his port [part] of Illinois — without ever having seen a steam-powered train. He had no idea, and yet he knew what it could be. Thirty years later, as President, Lincoln signed the law that built the first Transcontinental Railroad, uniting our country from ocean to ocean. Great President. Most people don't even know he was a Republican, right? Does anyone know? Lot of people don't know that. We have to build that up a little bit more. Let's take an ad — let's use one of those PACs. (Laughter.)

Those PACs, you never know what the hell is going to come out of those PACs. (Laughter.) You think they're friendly — although the best ad I ever had was one done against me by Hillary — it was so good, I said I hope she keeps running that ad. (Laughter.)

Another great Republican President, Dwight Eisenhower, had a vision of a national infrastructure plan. As an officer in the Army after World War I, he joined a military convoy that trekked across the nation to the Pacific Coast. It traveled along the Lincoln Highway — called then the Lincoln Highway. Its journey began by the South Lawn of the White House, at a monument known today as Zero Milestone. Anybody know where that is? The journey made a great impression on then young Eisenhower. More than three decades later, as President, he signed the bill that created our great Interstate Highway System — once again uniting us as a nation.

Now is time for a new Republican administration, working with our Republican Congress, to pass the next great infrastructure bill. (Applause.) Our party must dream as big and as bold as Lincoln and Eisenhower. Together, Republicans will lead America into our unbelievable future. We have so much potential. We have so much potential. I see it now even more than I saw it in this great campaign — which turned out to be a movement, a movement like the world has never seen before, actually.

You know, it's funny, I've said that so often, they don't even correct me — the fake media. They never correct me, because it's true. Oh, believe me, if it's off by 100th of a percent, it's like I end up getting Pinocchio's, right? They don't even correct me. One of the great movements of all time. And it's not my movement. It's a movement of the people. It's been something that's really been very special. I'm like a messenger. I'm nothing more than a messenger. (Applause.) I'm a messenger. I did a good job as a messenger, but I'm a messenger. It's been a lot of fun, too.

Imagine the breakthroughs that will breathe fresh life into forgotten places. Picture the new roads that will carve pathways all across our land — and we need them. And think of the new inventions that will lift up the sights of our nation.

Finally, as we imagine this new prosperity at home, let us also work to achieve real and enduring peace abroad. (Applause.) People don't realize, I have to say, what a mess we inherited. I'm telling you, you look at North Korea. You look at the Middle East. You look all over. You look at the horrible, horrible, horrible Iran deal. I still have not been able to figure out why anybody would have signed that deal. I asked generals — I have them in my office — I say, General, please tell me why did they sign that deal. Unbelievable. But we're going to straighten things out, folks.

The best Republican Presidents have not only been warfighters, but also peacemakers. We will never hesitate to do what we must to keep us safe today, but we will always seek a more peaceful tomorrow. We will, and we will succeed. (Applause.)

If we stand for these things — safety, prosperity and peace — then there is no limit to what we can achieve: A future where millions are lifted from welfare to work. And they're going to love it. They're going to love it. They're going to love waking up in the morning, going to work. Communities thriving with jobs and surging with commerce. Inner cities filled with new hope and new opportunity. Schools where our children can learn free from violence and free from fear. And new frontiers in science, technology and space that inspire the next generation of American youth.

All of this, and so much more, is possible. Our country is great. A new national pride is stirring our souls. A new optimism is sweeping our land. A new era of American greatness is just beginning.

Somewhere in America tonight, a child is born in poverty, looking up into the sky, and filling their heart with dreams — big, beautiful, bold dreams. And if we make the right choices together, then no one will ever have to tell that child that their dreams will have to wait for another day, another year, or another decade. Because the waiting now is over. The time for action is now. This is the moment when great deeds are done — and we will do those great deeds. By putting our faith in the people, and by putting our trust in God, we will rise to this occasion like no one has ever risen before. (Applause.)

Thank you so much. Thank you. Great people, great country. Thank you so much.

We will prove worthy of this moment. Anything is possible if we stand together, united and strong. Not just as Republicans — but as great and unified Americans. Join me in believing in this better and brighter future. Join me in building this reality. And join me in rededicating ourselves to the common good of this nation that we all love so much. Together, we will defend our freedoms. We will defend our people. And we will defend our great and beautiful American flag. (Applause.)

Thank you. God bless you, and God bless the United States of America. Thank you very much. (Applause.)

Remarks by the President in Nashville, Tennessee

President Donald Trump spoke at a Make American Great Again rally on March 15, 2017, in Nashville, Tennessee.

THE PRESIDENT: Thank you very much, everybody. Thank you. (Applause.) So we're just going to let the other folks come in, fill it up. This is some crowd. You have to see what's outside, you wouldn't even believe it. (Applause.) Unbelievable.

So I'm thrilled to be here in Nashville, Tennessee, the home — (applause) — of country music, Southern hospitality, and the great President Andrew Jackson. (Applause.) I just came from a tour of Andrew Jackson's home to mark the 250th anniversary of his birth. Jackson's life was devoted to one very crucial principle — he understood that real leadership means putting America first. (Applause.)

Before becoming President, Andrew Jackson served your state from the House of Representatives and in the United States Senate, and he also served as commander of the Tennessee militia. Tough cookie. Tough cookie. (Applause.)

So let's begin tonight by thanking all of the incredible men and women of the United States military and all of our wonderful veterans. The veterans. (Applause.)

AUDIENCE: USA! USA! USA!

THE PRESIDENT: Amazing. There's no place I'd rather be than with all of you here tonight, with the wonderful, hardworking citizens of our country. (Applause.) I would much rather spend time with you than any of the pundits, consultants, or special interests, certainly — or reporters from Washington, D.C. (Applause.)

It's patriotic Americans like you who make this country run, and run well. You pay your taxes, follow our laws, support your communities, raise your children, love your country, and send your bravest to fight in our wars. (Applause.) All you want is a government that shows you the same loyalty in return. It's time that Washington heard your voice — and believe me, on November 8th, they heard your voice. (Applause.) The forgotten men and women of our country will never be forgotten again, believe me. (Applause.)

I want to thank so many of your state leaders — State Party Chairman Scott Golden; Congressman Scott DesJarlais; Congresswoman Marsha Blackburn; Congresswoman Diane Black; Congressman Jimmy Duncan — right from the beginning. (Applause.) Governor Bill Haslam. (Applause.) A great friend of mine, Senator Bob Corker. (Applause.) An incredible guy, respected by all — Senator Lamar Alexander. (Applause.) And so many more. Thank you all for being here.

We're going to be working closely together to deliver for you, the citizens of Tennessee, like you've never been delivered for before. Thank you. Thank you. (Applause.) Thank you. We're going to reduce your taxes — big league. Big. (Applause.) Big. I want to start that process so quickly. Got to get the healthcare done. We got to start the tax reductions. (Applause.)

We are going to enforce our trade rules and bring back our jobs, which are scattered all over the world. They're coming back to our country. (Applause.) We're going to support the amazing — absolutely amazing men and women of law enforcement. (Applause.) Protect your freedoms, and defend the Second Amendment. (Applause.) And we are going to restore respect for our country and for its great and very beautiful flag. (Applause.)

It's been a little over 50 days since my inauguration, and we've been putting our America First agenda very much into action. You see what's happening. We're keeping our promises. In fact, they have signs — "He's Kept His Promise." They're all over the place. I have. (Applause.) We have done far more — I think maybe more than anybody's done in this office in 50 days, that I could tell you. (Applause.)

And we have just gotten started. Wait until you see what's coming, folks. We've appointed a Supreme Court justice to replace the late, great Antonin Scalia. His name is Judge Neil Gorsuch. (Applause.) He will uphold and defend the Constitution of the United States. We are proposing a budget that will shrink the bloated federal bureaucracy — and I mean bloated — while protecting our national security. You see what we're doing with our military — bigger, better, stronger than ever before. You see what's happening. (Applause.) And you're already seeing the results. Our budget calls for one of the single largest increases in defense spending history in this country. (Applause.)

We believe — especially the people in Tennessee, I know you people so well — (applause) — in peace through strength. That's what we're going to have. And we are taking steps to make sure that our allies pay their fair share. They have to pay. (Applause.) We've begun a dramatic effort to eliminate job-killing federal regulations like nobody has ever seen before — slash, slash. We're going to protect the environment, we're going to protect people's safeties, but, let me tell you, the regulation business has become a terrible business, and we're going to bring it down to where it should be. (Applause.)

AUDIENCE: USA! USA! USA!

THE PRESIDENT: Okay, let's go. One person — and they'll be the story tomorrow — did you hear there was a protestor? (Applause.)

We're going to put our miners back to work. We're going to put our auto industry back to work. Already because of this new business climate, we are creating jobs that are starting to pour back into our country like we haven't seen in many, many decades. (Applause.)

In the first two job reports since I took the oath of office, we've already added nearly half a million new jobs, and believe me, it's just beginning. (Applause.) I've already authorized the construction of the long-stalled and delayed Keystone and Dakota Access pipelines. (Applause.) A lot of jobs.

I've also directed that new pipelines must be constructed with American steel. (Applause.) They want to build them here, they use our steel. We believe in two simple rules: Buy American and Hire American. (Applause.)

On trade, I've kept my promise to the American people, and withdrawn from the Trans-Pacific Partnership disaster. (Applause.) Tennessee has lost one third of its manufacturing jobs since the institution of NAFTA, one of the worst trade deals ever in history. Our nation has lost over 60,000 factories since China joined the World Trade Organization — 60,000. Think of that. More than that.

We're not going to let it happen anymore. From now on, we are going to defend the American worker and our great American companies. (Applause.) And if America does what it says, and if your President does what I've been telling you, there is nobody anywhere in the world that can even come close to us, folks. Not even close. (Applause.)

If a company wants to leave America, fire their workers, and then ship their new products back into our country, there will be consequences. (Applause.) That's what we have borders for. And by the way, aren't our borders getting extremely strong? (Applause.) Very strong.

AUDIENCE: USA! USA! USA!

THE PRESIDENT: Don't even think about it. We will build the wall. Don't even think about it. (Applause.) In fact, as you probably read, we went out to bid. We had hundreds of bidders. Everybody wants to build our wall. (Applause.) Usually, that means we're going to get a good price. We're going to get a good price, believe me. (Applause.) We're going to build the wall.

Some of the fake news said, I don't think Donald Trump wants to build the wall. Can you imagine if I said we're not going to build a wall? Fake news. Fake, fake news. Fake news, folks. A lot of fake.

No, the wall is way ahead of schedule in terms of where we are. It's under design, and you're going to see some very good things happening. But the border by itself right now is doing very well. It's becoming very strong. General Kelly has done a great job — General Kelly.

My administration is also following through on our promise to secure, protect, and defend that border within our United States. Our southern border will be protected always. It will have the wall. Drugs will stop pouring in and poisoning our youth, and that will happen very, very soon. You're already seeing what's going on. The drugs are pouring into our country, folks. They are poisoning our youth and plenty of others, and we're going to stop it. We're not going to playing games. Not going to be playing games. (Applause.) Following my executive action — and don't forget, we've only been here for like — what? — 50 days — we've already experienced an unprecedented 40-percent reduction in illegal immigration on our Southern border; 61 percent since Inauguration Day — 61 percent. Think about it.

And now people are saying, we're not going to go there anymore because we can't get in. So it's going to get better and better. We got to stop those drugs, though. We got to stop those drugs.

During the campaign, as I traveled all across this country, I met with many American families whose loved ones were viciously and violently killed by illegal immigrants because our government refused to enforce our already existing laws. These American victims were ignored by the media. They were ignored by Washington. But they were not ignored by me, and they're not ignored by you, and they never will be ignored certainly any longer. Not going to happen. (Applause.)

As we speak, we are finding the drug dealers, the robbers, thieves, gang members, killers and criminals preying on our citizens. One by one — you're reading about it, right? They're being thrown out of our country. They're being thrown into prisons. And we will not let them back in. (Applause.)

We're also working, night and day, to keep our nation safe from terrorism. (Applause.) We have seen the devastation from 9/11 to Boston to San Bernardino — hundreds upon hundreds of people from outside our country have been convicted of terrorism-related offenses in the United States courts. Right now we have investigations going on all over — hundreds of refugees are under federal investigation for terrorism and related reasons. We have entire regions of the world destabilized by terrorism and ISIS. For this reason, I issued an executive order to temporarily suspend immigration from places where it cannot safely occur. (Applause.)

But let me give you the bad news. We don't like bad news, right? I don't want to hear — and I'll turn it into good. But let me give you the bad, the sad news. Moments ago, I learned that a district judge in Hawaii — part of the much overturned 9th Circuit Court — and I have to be nice; otherwise I'll get criticized for speaking poorly about our courts. I'll be criticized by these people, among the most dishonest people in the world — I will be criticized — I'll be criticized by them for speaking harshly about our courts. I would never want to do that. A judge has just blocked our executive order on travel and refugees coming into our country from certain countries.

AUDIENCE: Booo —

THE PRESIDENT: The order he blocked was a watered-version of the first order that was also blocked by another judge and should have never been blocked to start with. This new order was tailored to the dictates of the 9th Circuit's — in my opinion — flawed ruling. This is, the opinion of many, an unprecedented judicial overreach. The law and the Constitution give the President the power to suspend immigration when he deems — or she — or she. Fortunately, it will not be Hillary she. (Applause.) When he or she deems it to be in the national interest of our country.

So we have a lot of lawyers here. We also have a lot of smart people here. Let me read to you directly from the federal statute, 212F, of the immigration — and you know what I'm talking about, right? Can I read this to you? Listen to this. Now, we're all smart people. We're all good students — some are bad students, but even if you're a bad student this is a real easy one, let me tell you. Ready?

So here's the statute — which they don't even want to quote when they overrule it. And it was put here for the security of our country. And this goes beyond me, because there will be other Presidents, and we need this. And sometimes we need it very badly for security — security of our country.

It says — now, listen how easy this is. "Whenever the President finds that the entry of any aliens or any class of aliens would be detrimental to the interests of the United States, he may, by proclamation, and for such period as he — see, it wasn't politically correct, because it should say he or she. You know, today they'd say that. Actually, that's the only mistake they made. "as he shall deem necessary, suspending entry of all aliens, or any class of aliens, as immigrants or nonimmigrants, or pose on the entry of aliens any restrictions he may deems to be appropriate." In other words, if he thinks there's danger out there, he or she — whoever is President — can say, I'm sorry, folks, not now, please. We've got enough problems. (Applause.)

We're talking about the safety of our nation, the safety and security of our people. (Applause.) Now, I know you people aren't skeptical people because nobody would be that way in Tennessee.

Right? Nobody — not Tennessee. You don't think this was done by a judge for political reasons, do you? No.

AUDIENCE: Booo —

THE PRESIDENT: This ruling makes us look weak — which, by the way, we no longer are, believe me. (Applause.) Just look at our borders. We're going to fight this terrible ruling. We're going to take our case as far as it needs to go, including all the way up to the Supreme Court. (Applause.) We're going to win. We're going to keep our citizens safe. And regardless, we're going to keep our citizens safe, believe me. (Applause.) Even liberal Democratic lawyer, Alan Dershowitz —- good lawyer — just said that we would win this case before the Supreme Court of the United States. (Applause.)

Remember this, I wasn't thrilled, but the lawyers all said, let's tailor it. This is a watered–down version of the first one. This is a watered–down version. And let me tell you something, I think we ought to go back to the first one and go all the way, which is what I wanted to do in the first one. (Applause.)

The danger is clear, the law is clear, the need for my executive order is clear. I was elected to change our broken and dangerous system and thinking in government that has weakened and endangered our country and left our people defenseless. (Applause.) And I will not stop fighting for the safety of you and your families, believe me. Not today, not ever. We're going to win it. We're going to win it. (Applause.)

We're going to apply common sense. We're going to apply intelligence. And we're never quitting, and we're never going away, and we're never, ever giving up. The best way to keep foreign terrorists — or, as some people would say in certain instances, radical Islamic terrorists — from attacking our country is to stop them from entering our country in the first place. (Applause.)

We'll take it, but these are the problems we have. People are screaming, break up the 9th Circuit. And I'll tell you what, that 9th Circuit — you have to see. Take a look at how many times they have been overturned with their terrible decisions. Take a look. And this is what we have to live with.

Finally, I want to get to taxes. I want to cut the hell out of taxes, but — (applause) — but before I can do that — I would have loved to have put it first, I'll be honest — there is one more very important thing that we have to do, and we are going to repeal and replace horrible, disastrous Obamacare. (Applause.)

If we leave Obamacare in place, millions and millions of people will be forced off their plans, and your senators just told me that in your state you're down to practically no insurers. You're going to have nobody. You're going to have nobody. And this is true all over. The insurers are fleeing. The insurers are fleeing. It's a catastrophic situation, and there's nothing to compare anything to because Obamacare won't be around for a year or two. It's gone. So it's not like, oh, gee, they have this. Obamacare is gone.

Premiums will continue to soar double digits and even triple digits in many cases. It will drain our budget and destroy our jobs. Remember all of the broken promises? You can keep your doctor, you can keep your plan. Remember the wise guy — remember the wise guy that essentially said the American people — the so–called architect — the American people are stupid because they approved it? We're going to show them.

Those in Congress who made these promises have no credibility whatsoever on healthcare. (Applause.) And remember this — remember this: If we took, because there's such divisiveness — and I'm not just talking now, with me. There was with Obama. There was with Bush. The level of hatred and divisiveness with the politicians. I remember years ago, I'd go to Washington — I* was always very politically active — and Republicans and Democrats, they'd fight during the day and they go to dinner at night. Today, there's a level that nobody has seen before.

Just remember this: If we submitted the Democrats' plan, drawn everything perfect for the Democrats, we wouldn't get one vote from the Democrats. That's the way it is. That's how much divisiveness and other things there are. So it's a problem. But we're going to get it by.

So, I've met with so many victims of Obamacare —- the people who have been so horribly hurt by this horrible legislation. At the very core of Obamacare was a fatal flaw — the government forcing people to buy a government–approved product. There are very few people — very few people.

AUDIENCE MEMBER: Booo —

THE PRESIDENT: By the way — watch what happens. Now you just booed Obamacare. They will say, Trump got booed when he mentioned — they're bad people, folks. They're bad people.

AUDIENCE: Booo —

THE PRESIDENT: Tonight, I'll go home, I'll turn on, I'll say — listen, I'll turn on that television. My wife will say, darling, it's too bad you got booed. I said, I didn't get booed. This was a — I said, no, no, they were booing Obamacare. Watch, a couple of them will actually do it, almost guaranteed. But when we call them out, it makes it harder for them to do it. So we'll see. It's the fake, fake media. We want Americans to be able to purchase the health insurance plans they want, not the plans forced on them by our government. (Applause.)

The House has put forward a plan to repeal and replace Obamacare based on the principles I outlined in my joint address, but let me tell you, we're going to arbitrate, we're going to all get together and we're going to get something done. Remember this — if we didn't do it the way we're doing it, we need 60 votes so we have to get the Democrats involved. They won't vote, no matter what we do, they're not going to vote. So we're doing it a different way, a complex way. It's fine. The end result is when you have phase one, phase two, phase three — it's going to be great. It's going to be great.

And then, we get on to tax reductions, which I like. (Applause.) The House legislation does so much for you. It gives the states Medicaid flexibility. And some of the states will take over their healthcare. Governor Rick Scott in Florida said, just send me the money — they run a great plan. We have states that are doing great. It gives great flexibility.

Thank you, folks. Thank you. (Applause.) It repeals hundreds of billions of dollars in Obamacare taxes. It provides tax credits to purchase the care that is rightfully theirs. The bill that I will ultimately sign — and that will be a bill where everybody is going to get into the room and we're going to get it done — we'll get rid of Obamacare and make healthcare better for you and for your family. (Applause.)

And once this is done, and a step further, we are going to try and put it in phase three — I'm going to work on bringing down the cost of medicine by having a fair and competitive bidding process. (Applause.)

We welcome this healthcare debate and its negotiation, and we're going to carry it out, and have been carrying it out, in the full light of day — unlike the way Obamacare was passed. Remember, folks, if we don't do anything, Obamacare is gone. It's not like, oh, gee, it's going to be wonderful in three years. It's gone. It's gone. It's gone. Not working. It's gone. What we cannot do is to be intimidated by the dishonest attacks from Democratic leaders in Congress who broke the system in the first place and who don't believe you should be able to make your own healthcare decisions. (Applause.)

I am very confident that if we empower the American people we will accomplish incredible things for our country — not just on healthcare, but all across our government. We will unlock new frontiers in science and in medicine. We will give our children the right to attend the school of their choice, one where they will be taught to love this country and its values. (Applause.) We will create millions and millions of new jobs by lowering taxes on our businesses, and very importantly for our workers, we're going to lower taxes. (Applause.)

And we will fight for the right of every American child to grow up in a safe neighborhood, attend a great school, and to graduate with access to a high-paying job that they love doing. (Applause.)

No matter our background, no matter our income, no matter our geography, we all share the same home. We all salute the same flag. And we all are made by the same God. (Applause.)

AUDIENCE: USA! USA! USA!

THE PRESIDENT: It's time to embrace our glorious American destiny. Anything we can dream for our country we can achieve for our country. All we have to do is tap into that American pride that is swelling our hearts and stirring our souls. And we found that out very recently in our last election — a lot of pride. (Applause.) We are all Americans, and the future truly belongs to us. The future belongs to all of you. This is your moment. This is your time. This is the hour when history is made. All we have to do is put our own citizens first, and together we will make America strong again. (Applause.) We will make America wealthy again. We will make America proud again. We will make America safe again. And we will make America great again. (Applause.)

Thank you. God bless you. Thank you. (Applause.) God bless you, everybody. (Applause.)

Trump's Address to a Joint Session of Congress

This is an annotated transcript of a speech President Trump delivered to a joint session of Congress on Feb. 28, 2017.

THE PRESIDENT: Thank you very much. Mr. Speaker, Mr. Vice President, members of Congress, the First Lady of the United States — (applause) — and citizens of America:

Tonight, as we mark the conclusion of our celebration of Black History Month, we are reminded of our nation's path towards civil rights and the work that still remains to be done. (Applause.) Recent threats targeting Jewish community centers and vandalism of Jewish cemeteries, as well as last week's shooting in Kansas City, remind us that while we may be a nation divided on policies, we are a country that stands united in condemning hate and evil in all of its very ugly forms. (Applause.)

Each American generation passes the torch of truth, liberty and justice in an unbroken chain all the way down to the present. That torch is now in our hands. And we will use it to light up the world. I am here tonight to deliver a message of unity and strength, and it is a message deeply delivered from my heart. A new chapter — (applause) — of American Greatness is now beginning. A new national pride is sweeping across our nation. And a new surge of optimism is placing impossible dreams firmly within our grasp.

What we are witnessing today is the renewal of the American spirit. Our allies will find that America is once again ready to lead. (Applause.) All the nations of the world — friend or foe — will find that America is strong, America is proud, and America is free.

In nine years, the United States will celebrate the 250th
anniversary of our founding — 250 years since the day we
declared our independence. It will be one of the great milestones
in the history of the world. But what will America look like as we
reach our 250th year? What kind of country will we leave for our
children?

I will not allow the mistakes of recent decades past to define the
course of our future. For too long, we've watched our middle class
shrink as we've exported our jobs and wealth to foreign countries.
 We've financed and built one global project after another, but
ignored the fates of our children in the inner cities of Chicago,
Baltimore, Detroit, and so many other places throughout our land.

We've defended the borders of other nations while leaving our
own borders wide open for anyone to cross and for drugs to pour in
at a now unprecedented rate.

And we've spent trillions and trillions of dollars overseas, while
our infrastructure at home has so badly crumbled.

Then, in 2016, the Earth shifted beneath our feet. The rebellion
started as a quiet protest, spoken by families of all colors and
creeds — families who just wanted a fair shot for their children
and a fair hearing for their concerns.

But then the quiet voices became a loud chorus as thousands of
citizens now spoke out together, from cities small and large, all
across our country. Finally, the chorus became an earthquake, and
the people turned out by the tens of millions, and they were all
united by one very simple, but crucial demand: that America must
put its own citizens first. Because only then can we truly make
America great again. (Applause.)

Dying industries will come roaring back to life. Heroic veterans
will get the care they so desperately need. Our military will be
given the resources its brave warriors so richly deserve.
 Crumbling infrastructure will be replaced with new roads, bridges,
tunnels, airports and railways gleaming across our very, very

beautiful land. Our terrible drug epidemic will slow down and, ultimately, stop. And our neglected inner cities will see a rebirth of hope, safety and opportunity. Above all else, we will keep our promises to the American people. (Applause.)

It's been a little over a month since my inauguration, and I want to take this moment to update the nation on the progress I've made in keeping those promises.

Since my election, Ford, Fiat-Chrysler, General Motors, Sprint, Softbank, Lockheed, Intel, Walmart, and many others, have announced that they will invest billions of dollars in the United States and will create tens of thousands of new American jobs. (Applause.)

The stock market has gained almost $3 trillion in value since the election on November 8th, a record. We've saved taxpayers hundreds of millions of dollars by bringing down the price of a fantastic — and it is a fantastic — new F-35 jet fighter, and we'll be saving billions more on contracts all across our government. We have placed a hiring freeze on non-military and non-essential federal workers.

We have begun to drain the swamp of government corruption by imposing a five-year ban on lobbying by executive branch officials and a lifetime ban — (applause) — thank you — and a lifetime ban on becoming lobbyists for a foreign government.

We have undertaken a historic effort to massively reduce job-crushing regulations, creating a deregulation task force inside of every government agency. (Applause.) And we're imposing a new rule which mandates that for every one new regulation, two old regulations must be eliminated. (Applause.) We're going to stop the regulations that threaten the future and livelihood of our great coal miners. (Applause.)

We have cleared the way for the construction of the Keystone and Dakota Access Pipelines — (applause) — thereby creating tens of thousands of jobs. And I've issued a new directive that new American pipelines be made with American steel. (Applause.)

We have withdrawn the United States from the job-killing Trans-Pacific Partnership. (Applause.) And with the help of Prime Minister Justin Trudeau, we have formed a council with our neighbors in Canada to help ensure that women entrepreneurs have access to the networks, markets and capital they need to start a business and live out their financial dreams. (Applause.)

To protect our citizens, I have directed the Department of Justice to form a Task Force on Reducing Violent Crime. I have further ordered the Departments of Homeland Security and Justice, along with the Department of State and the Director of National Intelligence, to coordinate an aggressive strategy to dismantle the criminal cartels that have spread all across our nation. (Applause.) We will stop the drugs from pouring into our country and poisoning our youth, and we will expand treatment for those who have become so badly addicted. (Applause.)

At the same time, my administration has answered the pleas of the American people for immigration enforcement and border security. (Applause.) By finally enforcing our immigration laws, we will raise wages, help the unemployed, save billions and billions of dollars, and make our communities safer for everyone. (Applause.) We want all Americans to succeed, but that can't happen in an environment of lawless chaos. We must restore integrity and the rule of law at our borders. (Applause.)

For that reason, we will soon begin the construction of a great, great wall along our southern border. (Applause.) As we speak tonight, we are removing gang members, drug dealers, and criminals that threaten our communities and prey on our very innocent citizens. Bad ones are going out as I speak, and as I promised throughout the campaign.

To any in Congress who do not believe we should enforce our laws, I would ask you this one question: What would you say to the American family that loses their jobs, their income, or their loved one because America refused to uphold its laws and defend its borders? (Applause.)

Our obligation is to serve, protect, and defend the citizens of the United States. We are also taking strong measures to protect our nation from radical Islamic terrorism. (Applause.) According to data provided by the Department of Justice, the vast majority of individuals convicted of terrorism and terrorism-related offenses since 9/11 came here from outside of our country. We have seen the attacks at home — from Boston to San Bernardino to the Pentagon, and, yes, even the World Trade Center.

We have seen the attacks in France, in Belgium, in Germany, and all over the world.

It is not compassionate, but reckless, to allow uncontrolled entry from places where proper vetting cannot occur. Those given the high honor of admission to the United States should support this country and love its people and its values.

It is not compassionate, but reckless to allow uncontrolled entry from places where proper vetting cannot occur. (Applause.) Those given the high honor of admission to the United States should support this country and love its people and its values. We cannot allow a beachhead of terrorism to form inside America. We cannot allow our nation to become a sanctuary for extremists. (Applause.)

That is why my administration has been working on improved vetting procedures, and we will shortly take new steps to keep our nation safe and to keep out those out who will do us harm. (Applause.)

As promised, I directed the Department of Defense to develop a plan to demolish and destroy ISIS — a network of lawless savages that have slaughtered Muslims and Christians, and men, and women, and children of all faiths and all beliefs. We will work with our allies, including our friends and allies in the Muslim world, to extinguish this vile enemy from our planet. (Applause.)

I have also imposed new sanctions on entities and individuals who support Iran's ballistic missile program, and reaffirmed our unbreakable alliance with the State of Israel. (Applause.)

Finally, I have kept my promise to appoint a justice to the United States Supreme Court, from my list of 20 judges, who will defend our Constitution. (Applause.)

I am greatly honored to have Maureen Scalia with us in the gallery tonight. (Applause.) Thank you, Maureen. Her late, great husband, Antonin Scalia, will forever be a symbol of American justice. To fill his seat, we have chosen Judge Neil Gorsuch, a man of incredible skill and deep devotion to the law. He was confirmed unanimously by the Court of Appeals, and I am asking the Senate to swiftly approve his nomination. (Applause.)

Tonight, as I outline the next steps we must take as a country, we must honestly acknowledge the circumstances we inherited.

Ninety-four million Americans are out of the labor force. Over 43 million people are now living in poverty, and over 43 million Americans are on food stamps.

More than 1 in 5 people in their prime working years are not working.

We have the worst financial recovery in 65 years. In the last eight years, the past administration has put on more new debt than nearly all of the other Presidents combined.

We've lost more than one-fourth of our manufacturing jobs since NAFTA was approved, and we've lost 60,000 factories since China joined the World Trade Organization in 2001. Our trade deficit in goods with the world last year was nearly $800 billion dollars. And overseas we have inherited a series of tragic foreign policy disasters.

Solving these and so many other pressing problems will require us to work past the differences of party. It will require us to tap into the American spirit that has overcome every challenge throughout our long and storied history. But to accomplish our goals at home and abroad, we must restart the engine of the American economy — making it easier for companies to do business in the United States, and much, much harder for companies to leave our country. (Applause.)

Right now, American companies are taxed at one of the highest rates anywhere in the world. My economic team is developing historic tax reform that will reduce the tax rate on our companies so they can compete and thrive anywhere and with anyone. (Applause.) It will be a big, big cut.

At the same time, we will provide massive tax relief for the middle class. We must create a level playing field for American companies and our workers. We have to do it. (Applause.) Currently, when we ship products out of America, many other countries make us pay very high tariffs and taxes. But when foreign companies ship their products into America, we charge them nothing, or almost nothing.

I just met with officials and workers from a great American company, Harley-Davidson. In fact, they proudly displayed five of their magnificent motorcycles, made in the USA, on the front lawn of the White House. ((Laughter and applause.) And they wanted me to ride one and I said, "No, thank you." (Laughter.)

At our meeting, I asked them, how are you doing, how is business? They said that it's good. I asked them further, how are you doing with other countries, mainly international sales? They told me — without even complaining, because they have been so mistreated for so long that they've become used to it — that it's very hard to do business with other countries because they tax our goods at such a high rate. They said that in the case of another country, they taxed their motorcycles at 100 percent. They weren't even asking for a change. But I am. (Applause.)

I believe strongly in free trade but it also has to be fair trade. It's been a long time since we had fair trade. The first Republican

President, Abraham Lincoln, warned that the "abandonment of the protective policy by the American government… will produce want and ruin among our people." Lincoln was right — and it's time we heeded his advice and his words. (Applause.) I am not going to let America and its great companies and workers be taken advantage of us any longer. They have taken advantage of our country. No longer. (Applause.)

I am going to bring back millions of jobs. Protecting our workers also means reforming our system of legal immigration. (Applause.) The current, outdated system depresses wages for our poorest workers, and puts great pressure on taxpayers. Nations around the world, like Canada, Australia and many others, have a merit-based immigration system. (Applause.) It's a basic principle that those seeking to enter a country ought to be able to support themselves financially. Yet, in America, we do not enforce this rule, straining the very public resources that our poorest citizens rely upon.

According to the National Academy of Sciences, our current immigration system costs America's taxpayers many billions of dollars a year.

Switching away from this current system of lower-skilled immigration, and instead adopting a merit-based system, we will have so many more benefits. It will save countless dollars, raise workers' wages, and help struggling families — including immigrant families — enter the middle class. And they will do it quickly, and they will be very, very happy, indeed. (Applause.)

I believe that real and positive immigration reform is possible, as long as we focus on the following goals: To improve jobs and wages for Americans; to strengthen our nation's security; and to restore respect for our laws. If we are guided by the wellbeing of American citizens, then I believe Republicans and Democrats can work together to achieve an outcome that has eluded our country for decades. (Applause.)

Another Republican President, Dwight D. Eisenhower, initiated the last truly great national infrastructure program — the building of the Interstate Highway System. The time has come for a new program of national rebuilding. (Applause.) America has spent approximately six trillion dollars in the Middle East, all this while our infrastructure at home is crumbling. With this six trillion dollars we could have rebuilt our country – twice. And maybe even three times if we had people who had the ability to negotiate.

To launch our national rebuilding, I will be asking Congress to approve legislation that produces a $1 trillion investment in infrastructure of the United States — financed through both public and private capital — creating millions of new jobs. (Applause.) This effort will be guided by two core principles: buy American and hire American. (Applause.)

Tonight, I am also calling on this Congress to repeal and replace Obamacare — (applause) — with reforms that expand choice, increase access, lower costs, and, at the same time, provide better healthcare. (Applause.)

Mandating every American to buy government-approved health insurance was never the right solution for our country. (Applause.) The way to make health insurance available to everyone is to lower the cost of health insurance, and that is what we are going do. (Applause.)

Obamacare premiums nationwide have increased by double and triple digits. As an example, Arizona went up 116 percent last year alone. Governor Matt Bevin of Kentucky just said Obamacare is failing in his State — it is unsustainable and collapsing.

One-third of counties have only one insurer, and they are losing them fast. They are losing them so fast. They are leaving, and many Americans have no choice at all. There's no choice left. Remember when you were told that you could keep your doctor and keep your plan? We now know that all of those promises have been totally broken. Obamacare is collapsing, and we must act decisively to protect all Americans. (Applause.)

Action is not a choice, it is a necessity. So I am calling on all Democrats and Republicans in Congress to work with us to save Americans from this imploding Obamacare disaster. (Applause.)

Here are the principles that should guide the Congress as we move to create a better healthcare system for all Americans:

First, we should ensure that Americans with preexisting conditions have access to coverage, and that we have a stable transition for Americans currently enrolled in the healthcare exchanges. (Applause.)

Secondly, we should help Americans purchase their own coverage through the use of tax credits and expanded Health Savings Accounts — but it must be the plan they want, not the plan forced on them by our government. (Applause.)

Thirdly, we should give our great state governors the resources and flexibility they need with Medicaid to make sure no one is left out. (Applause.)

Fourth, we should implement legal reforms that protect patients and doctors from unnecessary costs that drive up the price of insurance, and work to bring down the artificially high price of drugs, and bring them down immediately. (Applause.)

And finally, the time has come to give Americans the freedom to purchase health insurance across state lines — (applause) — which will create a truly competitive national marketplace that will bring costs way down and provide far better care. So important.

Everything that is broken in our country can be fixed. Every problem can be solved. And every hurting family can find healing and hope.

Our citizens deserve this, and so much more — so why not join forces and finally get the job done, and get it done right? (Applause.) On this and so many other things, Democrats and

Republicans should get together and unite for the good of our country and for the good of the American people. (Applause.)

My administration wants to work with members in both parties to make childcare accessible and affordable, to help ensure new parents that they have paid family leave, to invest in women's health, and to promote clean air and clear water, and to rebuild our military and our infrastructure.

True love for our people requires us to find common ground, to advance the common good, and to cooperate on behalf of every American child who deserves a much brighter future.

An incredible young woman is with us this evening, who should serve as an inspiration to us all. Today is Rare Disease Day, and joining us in the gallery is a rare disease survivor, Megan Crowley. (Applause.)

Megan was diagnosed with Pompe disease, a rare and serious illness, when she was 15 months old. She was not expected to live past five. On receiving this news, Megan's dad, John, fought with everything he had to save the life of his precious child. He founded a company to look for a cure, and helped develop the drug that saved Megan's life. Today she is 20 years old and a sophomore at Notre Dame. (Applause.)

Megan's story is about the unbounded power of a father's love for a daughter. But our slow and burdensome approval process at the Food and Drug Administration keeps too many advances, like the one that saved Megan's life, from reaching those in need. If we slash the restraints, not just at the FDA but across our government, then we will be blessed with far more miracles just like Megan. (Applause.) In fact, our children will grow up in a nation of miracles.

But to achieve this future, we must enrich the mind and the souls of every American child. Education is the civil rights issue of our time. (Applause.) I am calling upon members of both parties to pass an education bill that funds school choice for disadvantaged youth, including millions of African American and Latino children. (Applause.) These families should be free to choose the public, private, charter, magnet, religious, or home school that is right for them. (Applause.)

Joining us tonight in the gallery is a remarkable woman, Denisha Merriweather. As a young girl, Denisha struggled in school and failed third grade twice. But then she was able to enroll in a private center for learning — a great learning center — with the help of a tax credit and a scholarship program.

Today, she is the first in her family to graduate, not just from high school, but from college. Later this year she will get her master's degree in social work. We want all children to be able to break the cycle of poverty just like Denisha. (Applause.)

But to break the cycle of poverty, we must also break the cycle of violence.

The murder rate in 2015 experienced its largest single-year increase in nearly half a century.

In Chicago, more than 4,000 people were shot last year alone, and the murder rate so far this year has been even higher. This is not acceptable in our society. (Applause.)

Every American child should be able to grow up in a safe community, to attend a great school, and to have access to a high-paying job. (Applause.) But to create this future, we must work with, not against — not against — the men and women of law enforcement. (Applause.) We must build bridges of cooperation and trust — not drive the wedge of disunity and, really, it's what it is, division. It's pure, unadulterated division. We have to unify.

Police and sheriffs are members of our community. They're friends and neighbors, they're mothers and fathers, sons and daughters — and they leave behind loved ones every day who worry about whether or not they'll come home safe and sound.

We must support the incredible men and women of law enforcement. (Applause.)

And we must support the victims of crime. I have ordered the Department of Homeland Security to create an office to serve American victims. The office is called VOICE — Victims of Immigration Crime Engagement. We are providing a voice to those who have been ignored by our media and silenced by special interests. (Applause.) Joining us in the audience tonight are four very brave Americans whose government failed them. Their names are Jamiel Shaw, Susan Oliver, Jenna Oliver, and Jessica Davis.

Jamiel's 17-year-old son was viciously murdered by an illegal immigrant gang member who had just been released from prison. Jamiel Shaw, Jr. was an incredible young man, with unlimited potential who was getting ready to go to college where he would have excelled as a great college quarterback. But he never got the chance. His father, who is in the audience tonight, has become a very good friend of mine. Jamiel, thank you. Thank you. (Applause.)

Also with us are Susan Oliver and Jessica Davis. Their husbands, Deputy Sheriff Danny Oliver and Detective Michael Davis, were slain in the line of duty in California. They were pillars of their community. These brave men were viciously gunned down by an illegal immigrant with a criminal record and two prior deportations. Should have never been in our country.

Sitting with Susan is her daughter, Jenna. Jenna, I want you to know that your father was a hero, and that tonight you have the love of an entire country supporting you and praying for you. (Applause.)

To Jamiel, Jenna, Susan and Jessica, I want you to know that we will never stop fighting for justice. Your loved ones will never, ever be forgotten. We will always honor their memory. (Applause.)

Finally, to keep America safe, we must provide the men and women of the United States military with the tools they need to prevent war — if they must — they have to fight and they only have to win. (Applause.)

I am sending Congress a budget that rebuilds the military, eliminates the defense sequester — (applause) — and calls for one of the largest increases in national defense spending in American history. My budget will also increase funding for our veterans. Our veterans have delivered for this nation, and now we must deliver for them. (Applause.)

The challenges we face as a nation are great, but our people are even greater. And none are greater or braver than those who fight for America in uniform. (Applause.)

We are blessed to be joined tonight by Carryn Owens, the widow of a U.S. Navy Special Operator, Senior Chief William "Ryan" Owens. Ryan died as he lived: a warrior and a hero, battling against terrorism and securing our nation. (Applause.) I just spoke to our great General Mattis, just now, who reconfirmed that — and I quote — "Ryan was a part of a highly successful raid that generated large amounts of vital intelligence that will lead to many more victories in the future against our enemies." Ryan's legacy is etched into eternity. Thank you. (Applause.) And Ryan is looking down, right now — you know that — and he is very happy because I think he just broke a record. (Laughter and applause.)

For as the Bible teaches us, "There is no greater act of love than to lay down one's life for one's friends." Ryan laid down his life for his friends, for his country, and for our freedom. And we will never forget Ryan. (Applause.)

To those allies who wonder what kind of a friend America will be, look no further than the heroes who wear our uniform. Our foreign policy calls for a direct, robust and meaningful engagement with the world. It is American leadership based on vital security interests that we share with our allies all across the globe.

We strongly support NATO, an alliance forged through the bonds of two world wars that dethroned fascism, and a Cold War, and defeated communism. (Applause.)

But our partners must meet their financial obligations. And now, based on our very strong and frank discussions, they are beginning to do just that. In fact, I can tell you, the money is pouring in. Very nice. (Applause.) We expect our partners — whether in NATO, the Middle East, or in the Pacific — to take a direct and meaningful role in both strategic and military operations, and pay their fair share of the cost. Have to do that.

We will respect historic institutions, but we will respect the foreign rights of all nations, and they have to respect our rights as a nation also. (Applause.) Free nations are the best vehicle for expressing the will of the people, and America respects the right of all nations to chart their own path. My job is not to represent the world. My job is to represent the United States of America. (Applause.)

But we know that America is better off when there is less conflict, not more. We must learn from the mistakes of the past. We have seen the war and the destruction that have ravaged and raged throughout the world — all across the world. The only long-term solution for these humanitarian disasters, in many cases, is to create the conditions where displaced persons can safely return home and begin the long, long process of rebuilding. (Applause.)

America is willing to find new friends, and to forge new partnerships, where shared interests align. We want harmony and stability, not war and conflict. We want peace, wherever peace can be found.

America is friends today with former enemies. Some of our closest allies, decades ago, fought on the opposite side of these terrible, terrible wars. This history should give us all faith in the possibilities for a better world. Hopefully, the 250th year for America will see a world that is more peaceful, more just, and more free.

On our 100th anniversary, in 1876, citizens from across our nation came to Philadelphia to celebrate America's centennial. At that celebration, the country's builders and artists and inventors showed off their wonderful creations. Alexander Graham Bell displayed his telephone for the first time. Remington unveiled the first typewriter. An early attempt was made at electric light. Thomas Edison showed an automatic telegraph and an electric pen. Imagine the wonders our country could know in America's 250th year. (Applause.)

Think of the marvels we can achieve if we simply set free the dreams of our people. Cures to the illnesses that have always plagued us are not too much to hope. American footprints on distant worlds are not too big a dream.

Millions lifted from welfare to work is not too much to expect.

And streets where mothers are safe from fear, schools where children learn in peace, and jobs where Americans prosper and grow are not too much to ask. (Applause.)

When we have all of this, we will have made America greater than ever before — for all Americans. This is our vision. This is our mission. But we can only get there together. We are one people, with one destiny. We all bleed the same blood. We all salute the same great American flag. And we all are made by the same God. (Applause.)

When we fulfill this vision, when we celebrate our 250 years of glorious freedom, we will look back on tonight as when this new chapter of American Greatness began. The time for small thinking is over. The time for trivial fights is behind us. We just need the courage to share the dreams that fill our hearts, the bravery to express the hopes that stir our souls, and the confidence to turn those hopes and those dreams into action.

From now on, America will be empowered by our aspirations, not burdened by our fears; inspired by the future, not bound by the failures of the past; and guided by our vision, not blinded by our doubts.

I am asking all citizens to embrace this renewal of the American spirit. I am asking all members of Congress to join me in dreaming big, and bold, and daring things for our country. I am asking everyone watching tonight to seize this moment. Believe in yourselves, believe in your future, and believe, once more, in America.

Thank you, God bless you, and God bless the United States. (Applause.)

President Trump Press Conference

This is an annotated transcript of a press conference held by President Trump on Feb. 16, 2017, in the East Room at the White House.

THE PRESIDENT: Thank you very much. I just wanted to begin by mentioning that the nominee for Secretary of the Department of Labor will be Mr. Alex Acosta. He has a law degree from Harvard Law School, was a great student. Former clerk for Justice Samuel Alito. And he has had a tremendous career. He's a member, and has been a member, of the National Labor Relations Board, and has been through Senate confirmation three times, confirmed — did very, very well. And so Alex, I've wished him the best. We just spoke. And he's going to be — I think he'll be a tremendous Secretary of Labor.

And also, as you probably heard just a little while ago, Mick Mulvaney, former congressman, has just been approved — weeks late, I have to say that. Weeks, weeks late. Office of Management and Budget. And he will be, I think, a fantastic addition. Paul Singer has just left. As you know, Paul was very much involved with the anti-Trump, or, as they say, "Never Trump." And Paul just left and he's given us his total support. And it's all about unification. We're unifying the party, and hopefully we're going to be able to unify the country. It's very important to me. I've been talking about that for a long time, but it's very, very important to me. So I want to thank Paul Singer for being here and for coming up to the office. He was a very strong opponent, and now he's a very strong ally. And I appreciate that.

I think I'll say a few words, and then we'll take some questions.
And I had this time — we've been negotiating a lot of different
transactions to save money on contracts that were terrible,
including airplane contracts that were out of control and late and
terrible. Just absolutely catastrophic in terms of what was
happening. And we've done some really good work. We're very
proud of that.

And then right after that, you prepare yourselves and we'll do
some questions — unless you have no questions. That's always a
possibility.

I'm here today to update the American people on the incredible
progress that has been made in the last four weeks since my
inauguration. We have made incredible progress. I don't think
there's ever been a President elected who, in this short period of
time, has done what we've done.

A new Rasmussen poll, in fact — because the people get it; much
of the media doesn't get it. They actually get it, but they don't
write it — let's put it that way. But a new Rasmussen poll just
came out just a very short while ago, and it has our approval rating
at 55 percent and going up. The stock market has hit record
numbers, as you know. And there has been a tremendous surge of
optimism in the business world, which is — to me means
something much different than it used to. It used to mean, oh,
that's good. Now it means that's good for jobs. Very different.
Plants and factories are already starting to move back into the
United States and big league — Ford, General Motors, so many of
them.

I'm making this presentation directly to the American people with
the media present, which is an honor to have you this morning,
because many of our nation's reporters and folks will not tell you
the truth and will not treat the wonderful people of our country
with the respect that they deserve. And I hope going forward we
can be a little bit different, and maybe get along a little bit better, if
that's possible. Maybe it's not, and that's okay too.

Unfortunately, much of the media in Washington, D.C., along with New York, Los Angeles, in particular, speaks not for the people but for the special interests and for those profiting off a very, very obviously broken system. The press has become so dishonest that if we don't talk about it, we are doing a tremendous disservice to the American people — tremendous disservice. We have to talk about it to find out what's going on, because the press honestly is out of control. The level of dishonesty is out of control.

I ran for President to represent the citizens of our country. I am here to change the broken system so it serves their families and their communities well. I am talking, and really talking, on this very entrenched power structure, and what we're doing is we're talking about the power structure, we're talking about its entrenchment. As a result, the media is going through what they have to go through to oftentimes distort — not all the time — and some of the media is fantastic, I have to say; they're honest and fantastic. But much of it is not — the distortion. And we'll talk about it, and you'll be able to ask me questions about it.

But we're not going to let it happen, because I'm here again to take my message straight to the people. As you know, our administration inherited many problems across government and across the economy. To be honest, I inherited a mess — it's a mess — at home and abroad. A mess. Jobs are pouring out of the country. You see what's going on with all of the companies leaving our country, going to Mexico and other places — low-pay, low-wages. Mass instability overseas, no matter where you look. The Middle East, a disaster. North Korea — we'll take care of it, folks. We're going to take care of it all. I just want to let you know I inherited a mess.

Beginning on day one, our administration went to work to tackle these challenges. On foreign affairs, we've already begun enormously productive talks with many foreign leaders — much of it you've covered — to move forward toward stability, security, and peace in the most troubled regions of the world, which there are many.

We've had great conversations with the United Kingdom — and meetings — Israel, Mexico, Japan, China, and Canada. Really, really productive conversations. I would say far more productive than you would understand. We've even developed a new council with Canada to promote women's business leaders and entrepreneurs. It's very important to me, very important to my daughter Ivanka.

I have directed our defense community, headed by our great general, now Secretary Mattis — he's over there now, working very hard — to submit a plan for the defeat of ISIS, a group that celebrates the murder and torture of innocent people in large sections of the world. It used to be a small group, and now it's in large sections of the world. They've spread like cancer. ISIS has spread like cancer. Another mess I inherited.

And we have imposed new sanctions on the nation of Iran, who's totally taken advantage of our previous administration. And they're the world's top sponsor of terrorism. And we're not going to stop until that problem is properly solved. And it's not properly solved now. It's one of the worst agreements I've ever seen drawn by anybody.

I've ordered plans to begin for the massive rebuilding of the United States military. I've had great support from the Senate. I've had great support from Congress generally. We've pursued this rebuilding in the hopes that we will never have to use this military. And I will tell you that is my — I would be so happy if we never had to use it. But our country will never have had a military like the military we're about to build and rebuild. We have the greatest people on Earth in our military, but they don't have the right equipment. And their equipment is old. I used it, I talked about it at every stop. Depleted — it's depleted. It won't be depleted for long.

And I think one of the reasons I'm standing here instead of other people is that, frankly, I talked about we have to have a strong military. We have to have strong law enforcement also. So we do not go abroad in the search of war. We really are searching for peace, but it's peace through strength.

At home, we have begun the monumental task of returning the government back to the people on a scale not seen in many, many years. In each of these actions, I'm keeping my promises to the American people. These are campaign promises. Some people are so surprised that we're having strong borders. Well, that's what I've been talking about for a year and a half — strong borders. They're so surprised — "oh, you're having strong borders." Well, that's what I've been talking about to the press and to everybody else.

One promise after another after years of politicians lying to you to get elected. They lie to the American people in order to get elected. Some of the things I'm doing probably aren't popular, but they're necessary for security and for other reasons. And then coming to Washington and pursuing their own interests, which is more important to many politicians.

I'm here following through on what I pledged to do. That's all I'm doing. I put it out before the American people. Got 306 Electoral College votes. I wasn't supposed to get 222. They said there's no way to get 222; 230 is impossible. Two hundred and seventy, which you need, that was laughable. We got 306 because people came out and voted like they've never seen before. So that's the way it goes. I guess it was the biggest Electoral College win since Ronald Reagan.

In other words, the media is trying to attack our administration because they know we are following through on pledges that we made, and they're not happy about it for whatever reason. But a lot of people are happy about it. In fact, I'll be in Melbourne, Florida, five o'clock on Saturday, and I heard — just heard that the crowds are massive that want to be there.

I turn on the TV, open the newspapers, and I see stories of chaos. Chaos! Yet, it is the exact opposite. This administration is running like a fine-tuned machine, despite the fact that I can't get my Cabinet approved, and they're outstanding people. Like Senator Dan Coates whose there — one of the most respected men of the Senate — he can't get approved. How do you not approve him?

He's been a colleague, highly respected — brilliant guy, great guy, everybody knows it — but waiting for approval.

So we have a wonderful group of people that's working very hard, that's being very much misrepresented about, and we can't let that happen. So if the Democrats, who have — all you have to do is look at where they are right now — the only thing they can do is delay, because they've screwed things up royally, believe me.

Let me list to you some of the things that we've done in just a short period of time. I just got here. I got here with no Cabinet. Again, each of these actions is a promise I made to the American people. So we'll go over just some of them, and we have a lot happening next week and in the weeks coming. We've withdrawn from the job-killing disaster known as Trans-Pacific Partnership. We're going to make trade deals, but we're going to have one-on-one deals — bilateral. We're going to have one-on-one deals.

We've directed the elimination of regulations that undermine manufacturing, and called for expedited approval of the permits needed for America and American infrastructure, and that means plants, equipment, roads, bridges, factories. People take 10, 15, 20 years to get disapproved for a factory. They go in for a permit — it's many, many years. And then at the end of the process — they spend tens of millions of dollars on nonsense — and at the end of the process, they get rejected. Now, they may be rejected with me, but it's going to be a quick rejection. It's not going to take years. But mostly, it's going to be an acceptance. We want plants built, and we want factories built, and we want the jobs. We don't want the jobs going to other countries.

We've imposed a hiring freeze on nonessential federal workers. We've imposed a temporary moratorium on new federal regulations. We've issued a game-changing new rule that says for each one new regulation, two old regulations must be eliminated. Makes sense. Nobody has ever seen regulations like we have. If you go to other countries and you look at industries they have, and you say, let me see your regulations, and they're a fraction, just a tiny fraction of what we have. And I want regulations because I want safety, I want all environmental situations to be taken properly care of. It's very important to me. But you don't need four or five or six regulations to take care of the same thing.

We've stood up for the men and women of law enforcement, directing federal agencies to ensure they are protected from crimes of violence. We've directed the creation of a task force for reducing violent crime in America, including the horrendous situation — take a look at Chicago and others — taking place right now in our inner cities. Horrible. We've ordered the Department of Homeland Security and Justice to coordinate on a plan to destroy criminal cartels coming into the United States with drugs. We're becoming a drug-infested nation. Drugs are becoming cheaper than candy bars, and we're not going to let it happen any longer.

We've undertaken the most substantial border security measures in a generation to keep our nation and our tax dollars safe, and are now in the process of beginning to build a promised wall on the southern border. Met with General, now Secretary, Kelly yesterday and we're starting that process. And the wall is going to be a great wall, and it's going to be a wall negotiated by me. The price is going to come down, just like it has on everything else I've negotiated for the government. And we're going to have a wall that works. We're not going to have a wall like they have now, which is either nonexistent or a joke.

We've ordered a crackdown on sanctuary cities that refuse to comply with federal law and that harbor criminal aliens, and we've ordered an end to the policy of catch and release on the border. No more release, no matter who you are — release. We've begun a nationwide effort to remove criminal aliens, gang members, drug dealers, and others who pose a threat to public safety. We are saving American lives every single day. The court system has not made it easy for us. And we've even created a new office in Homeland Security dedicated to the forgotten American victims of illegal immigrant violence, of which there are many.

We've taken decisive action to keep radical Islamic terrorists out of our country. Though parts of our necessary and constitutional actions were blocked by a judge's, in my opinion, incorrect and unsafe ruling, our administration is working night and day to keep you safe — including reporters safe — and is vigorously defending this lawful order. I will not back down from defending our country. I got elected on defense of our country. And I keep my campaign promises. And our citizens will be very happy when they see the result. They already are. I can tell you that.

Extreme vetting will be put in place, and it already is in place in many places. In fact, we had to go quicker than we thought because of the bad decision we received from a circuit that has been overturned at a record number. I've heard 80 percent — I find that hard to believe; that's just a number I heard — that they're overturned 80 percent of the time. I think that circuit is in chaos and that circuit is, frankly, in turmoil. But we are appealing that and we are going further.

We're issuing a new executive action next week that will comprehensively protect our country, so we'll be going along the one path and hopefully winning that. At the same time, we will be issuing a new and very comprehensive order to protect our people, and that will be done some time next week, toward the beginning or middle at the latest part.

We've also taken steps to begin construction of the Keystone Pipeline and Dakota Access Pipelines — thousands and thousands of jobs — and put new "Buy American" measures in place to require American steel for American pipelines. In other words, they build a pipeline in this country and we use the powers of government to make that pipeline happen. We want them to use American steel. And they're willing to do that, but nobody ever asked before I came along. Even this order was drawn and they didn't say that. And I'm reading the order, I'm saying, why aren't we using American steel? And they said, that's a good idea. We put it in.

To drain the swamp of corruption in Washington, D.C. I've started by imposing a five-year lobbying ban on White House officials and a lifetime ban on lobbying for a foreign government. We've begun preparing to repeal and replace Obamacare. Obamacare is a disaster, folks. It's a disaster. You can say, oh, Obamacare — I mean, they fill up our alleys with people that you wonder how they get there, but they're not the Republican people that our representatives are representing. So we've begun preparing to repeal and replace Obamacare and are deep in the midst of negotiations on a very historic tax reform to bring our jobs back. We're bringing our jobs back to this country big league. It's already happening, but big league.

I've also worked to install a Cabinet over the delays and obstruction of Senate Democrats. You've seen what they've done over the last long number of years. That will be one of the great Cabinets ever assembled in American history. You look at Rex Tillerson — he's out there negotiating right now. General Mattis I mentioned before, General Kelly. We have great, great people. Mick is with us now. We have great people.

Among their responsibilities will be ending the bleeding of jobs from our country and negotiating fair trade deals for our citizens. Now, look, fair trade — not free — fair. If a country is taking advantage of us, we're not going to let that happen anymore. Every country takes advantage of us, almost. I may be able to find a couple that don't. But for the most part, that would be a very tough job for me to do.

Jobs have already started to surge. Since my election, Ford announced it will abandon its plans to build a new factory in Mexico and will instead invest $700 million in Michigan, creating many, many jobs. Fiat-Chrysler announced it will invest $1 billion in Ohio and Michigan, creating 2,000 new American jobs. They were with me a week ago. You know — you were here. General Motors, likewise, committed to invest billions of dollars in its American manufacturing operation, keeping many jobs here that were going to leave. And if I didn't get elected, believe me, they would have left. And these jobs and these things that I'm announcing would never have come here.

Intel just announced that it will move ahead with a new plant in Arizona that probably was never going to move ahead with. And that will result in at least 10,000 American jobs. Walmart announced it will create 10,000 jobs in the United States just this year because of our various plans and initiatives. There will be many, many more. Many more. These are a few that we're naming.

Other countries have been taking advantage of us for decades — decades and decades and decades, folks. And we're not going to let that happen anymore. Not going to let it happen.

And one more thing. I have kept my promise to the American people by nominating a justice of the United States Supreme Court, Judge Neil Gorsuch, who is from my list of 20, and who will be a true defender of our laws and our Constitution — highly respected, should get the votes from the Democrats — you may not see that, but he'll get there one way or the other. But he should get there the old-fashioned way, and he should get those votes.

This last month has represented an unprecedented degree of action on behalf of the great citizens of our country. Again, I say it — there has never been a presidency that's done so much in such a short period of time. And we haven't even started the big work that starts early next week. Some very big things are going to be announced next week.

So we're just getting started. We will be giving a speech, as I said, in Melbourne, Florida, at 5:00 p.m. I hope to see you there. And with that, I'd just say, God bless America, and let's take some questions.

Mara. Mara, go ahead. You were cut off pretty violently at our last news conference.

Q Did you fire Mike Flynn?

THE PRESIDENT: Mike Flynn is a fine person, and I asked for his resignation. He respectfully gave it. He is a man who — there was a certain amount of information given to Vice President

Pence, who is with us today. And I was not happy with the way that information was given.

He didn't have to do that, because what he did wasn't wrong, what he did in terms of the information he saw. What was wrong was the way that other people, including yourselves in this room, were given that information, because that was classified information that was given illegally. That's the real problem. And you can talk all you want about Russia, which was all a fake news, fabricated deal to try and make up for the loss of the Democrats, and the press plays right into it. In fact, I saw a couple of the people that were supposedly involved with all of this — they know nothing about it. They weren't in Russia, they never made a phone call to Russia, they never received a phone call. It's all fake news. It's all fake news.

The nice thing is I see it starting to turn, where people are now looking at the illegal, Mara — and I think it's very important — the illegal giving out classified information. And let me just tell you, it was given out, like, so much. I'll give you an example. I called, as you know, Mexico. It was a very confidential, classified call, but I called Mexico. And in calling Mexico, I figured, oh, well, that's — I spoke to the President of Mexico, had a good call. All of a sudden it's out for the world to see. It's supposed to be secret. It's supposed to be either confidential or classified in that case. Same thing with Australia. All of a sudden people are finding out exactly what took place.

The same thing happened with respect to General Flynn. Everybody saw this, and I'm saying — the first thing I thought of when I heard about it is, how does the press get this information that's classified? How do they do it? You know why? Because it's an illegal process, and the press should be ashamed of themselves. But, more importantly, the people that gave out the information to the press should be ashamed of themselves. Really ashamed.

Yes, go ahead.

Q Why did you keep your Vice President in the dark for almost two weeks?

THE PRESIDENT: Because when I looked at the information, I said, I don't think he did anything wrong. If anything, he did something right. He was coming into office, he looked at the information. He said, huh, that's fine, that's what they're supposed to do. They're supposed to be — and he didn't just call Russia. He called and spoke to, both ways — I think there were 30-some-odd countries. He's doing the job.

You know, he was just doing his job. The thing is he didn't tell our Vice President properly, and then he said he didn't remember. So either way, it wasn't very satisfactory to me. And I have somebody that I think will be outstanding for the position, and that also helps, I think, in the making of my decision.

But he didn't tell the Vice President of the United States the facts, and then he didn't remember. And that just wasn't acceptable to me.

Yes.

Q President Trump, since you brought up Russia, I'm looking for some clarification here. During the campaign, did anyone from your team communicate with members of the Russian government or Russian intelligence? And if so, what was the nature of those conversations?

THE PRESIDENT: Well, the failing New York Times wrote a big, long front-page story yesterday. And it was very much discredited, as you know. It was — it's a joke. And the people mentioned in the story — I notice they were on television today saying they never even spoke to Russia. They weren't even a part, really — I mean, they were such a minor part — I hadn't spoken to them. I think the one person, I don't think I've ever spoken to him. I don't think I've ever met him. And he actually said he was a very low-level member of, I think, a committee for a short period of time. I don't think I ever met him. Now, it's possible that I walked into a room and he was sitting there, but I don't think I ever met him. I didn't talk to him, ever. And he thought it was a joke.

The other person said he never spoke to Russia, never received a call. Look at his phone records, et cetera, et cetera. And the other person, people knew that he'd represented various countries, but I don't think he represented Russia — but knew that he represented various countries. That's what he does. I mean, people know that. That's Mr. Manafort, who's, by the way — who's, by the way, a respected man. He's a respected man. But I think he represented the Ukraine, or Ukraine government, or somebody. But everybody — people knew that. Everybody knew that. So these people — and he said that he has absolutely nothing to do and never has with Russia. And he said that very forcefully. I saw his statement. He said it very forcefully. Most of the papers don't print it because that's not good for their stories.

So the three people that they talked about all totally deny it. And I can tell you, speaking for myself, I own nothing in Russia. I have no loans in Russia. I don't have any deals in Russia. President Putin called me up very nicely to congratulate me on the win of the election. He then called me up extremely nicely to congratulate me on the inauguration, which was terrific. But so did many other leaders — almost all other leaders from almost all other countries. So that's the extent.

Russia is fake news. Russia — this is fake news put out by the media. The real news is the fact that people, probably from the Obama administration because they're there — because we have our new people going in place right now. As you know, Mike Pompeo is now taking control of the CIA. James Comey at FBI. Dan Coats is waiting to be approved. I mean, he is a senator, and a highly respected one. And he's still waiting to be approved. But our new people are going in.

And just while you're at, because you mentioned this, Wall Street Journal did a story today that was almost as disgraceful as the failing New Times's story yesterday. And it talked about — you saw it, front page. So, Director of National Intelligence just put out

— acting — a statement: "Any suggestion that the United States intelligence community" — this was just given to us — "is withholding information and not providing the best possible intelligence to the President and his national security team is not true."

So they took this front-page story out of The Wall Street Journal — top — and they just wrote the story is not true. And I'll tell you something, I'll be honest — because I sort of enjoy this back and forth, and I guess I have all my life, but I've never seen more dishonest media than, frankly, the political media. I thought the financial media was much better, much more honest. But I will say that I never get phone calls from the media. How do they write a story like that in The Wall Street Journal without asking me? Or how do they write a story in The New York Times, put it on front page? That was like that story they wrote about the women and me — front page. Big massive story. And it was nasty.

And then they called. They said, "We never said that. We like Mr. Trump." They called up my office — we like Mr. Trump; we never said that. And it was totally — they totally misrepresented those very wonderful women, I have to tell you — totally misrepresented. I said, give us a retraction. They never gave us a retraction. And, frankly, I then went on to other things.

Go ahead.

Q Mr. President —

THE PRESIDENT: You okay?

Q I am. Just wanted to get untangled. Very simply, you said today that you had the biggest electoral margins since Ronald Reagan with 304 or 306 electoral votes. In fact, President Obama got 365 in 2008.

THE PRESIDENT: Well, I'm talking about Republican. Yes.

Q President Obama, 332. George H.W. Bush, 426 when he won as President. So why should Americans trust —

THE PRESIDENT: Well, no, I was told — I was given that information. I don't know. I was just given. We had a very, very big margin.

Q I guess my question is, why should Americans trust you when you have accused the information they receive of being fake when you're providing information that's fake?

THE PRESIDENT: Well, I don't know. I was given that information. I was given — actually, I've seen that information around. But it was a very substantial victory. Do you agree with that?

Q You're the President.

THE PRESIDENT: Okay, thank you. That's a good answer. Yes.

Q Mr. President, thank you so much. Can you tell us in determining that Lieutenant General Flynn — there was no wrongdoing in your mind, what evidence was weighed? Did you have the transcripts of these telephone intercepts with Russian officials, particularly Ambassador Kislyak, who he was communicating with? What evidence did you weigh to determine there was no wrong doing?

And further than that, sir, you've said on a couple of occasions this morning that you were going to aggressively pursue the sources of these leaks.

THE PRESIDENT: We are.

Q Can we ask what you're doing to do? And also, we've heard about a review of the intelligence community headed by Stephen Feinberg. What can you tell us about that?

THE PRESIDENT: Well, first of all, about that, we now have Dan Coats, hopefully soon Mike Pompeo and James Comey, and they're in position. So I hope that we'll be able to straighten that out without using anybody else. The gentleman you mentioned is a very talented man, very successful man. And he has offered his services, and it's something we may take advantage of. But I don't think we'll need that at all because of the fact that I think that we're going to be able to straighten it out very easily on its own.

As far as the general is concerned, when I first heard about it, I said, huh, that doesn't sound wrong. My counsel came — Don McGahn, White House Counsel — and he told me, and I asked him, and he can speak very well for himself. He said he doesn't think anything is wrong. He really didn't think — it was really what happened after that, but he didn't think anything was done wrong. I didn't either, because I waited a period of time and I started to think about it. I said, well, I don't see — to me, he was doing the job.

The information was provided by — who I don't know — Sally Yates — and I was a little surprised because I said, doesn't sound like he did anything wrong there. But he did something wrong with respect to the Vice President, and I thought that was not acceptable. As far as the actual making the call — in fact, I've watched various programs and I've read various articles where he was just doing his job. That was very normal. At first, everybody got excited because they thought he did something wrong. After they thought about it, it turned out he was just doing his job.

So — and I do — and, by the way, with all of that being said, I do think he's a fine man.

Yes, Jon.

Q On the leaks, sir —

THE PRESIDENT: Go ahead, finish off, then I'll get you, Jon.

Q Sorry, what will you do on the leaks? You have said twice today —

THE PRESIDENT: Yes, we're looking at it very, very seriously. I've gone to all of the folks in charge of the various agencies, and we're — I've actually called the Justice Department to look into the leaks. Those are criminal leaks. They're put out by people either in agencies. I think you'll see it stopping because now we have our people in. You know, again, we don't have our people in because we can't get them approved by the Senate. We just had Jeff Sessions approved in Justice, as an example. So we are looking into that very seriously. It's a criminal act.

You know what I say — when I was called out on Mexico, I was shocked. Because all this equipment, all this incredible phone equipment. When I was called out on Mexico, I was — honestly, I was really, really surprised. But I said, you know, it doesn't make sense, that won't happen. But that wasn't that important to call, it was fine. I could show it to the world and he could show it to the world — the President who is a very fine man, by the way. Same thing with Australia. I said, that's terrible that it was leaked but it wasn't that important. But then I said, what happens when I'm dealing with the problem of North Korea? What happens when I'm dealing with the problems in the Middle East? Are you folks going to be reporting all of that very, very confidential information — very important, very — I mean, at the highest level, are you going to be reporting about that too?

So I don't want classified information getting out to the public. And in a way, that was almost a test. So I'm dealing with Mexico. I'm dealing with Argentina. We were dealing on this case with Mike Flynn. All this information gets put into the Washington Post and gets put into the New York Times. And I'm saying, what's going to happen when I'm dealing on the Middle East? What's going to happen when I'm dealing with really, really important subjects like North Korea? We've got to stop it. That's why it's a criminal penalty.

Yes, Jon.

Q Thank you, Mr. President. I just want to get you to clarify just a very important point. Can you say definitively that nobody on your campaign had any contacts with the Russians during the campaign? And, on the leaks, is it fake news or are these real leaks?

THE PRESIDENT: Well, the leaks are real. You're the one that wrote about them and reported them. I mean, the leaks are real. You know what they said — you saw it. And the leaks are absolutely real. The news is fake because so much of the news is fake.

So one thing that I felt it was very important to do — and I hope we can correct it, because there is nobody I have more respect for — well, maybe a little bit — than reporters, than good reporters. It's very important to me, and especially in this position. It's very important. I don't mind bad stories. I can handle a bad story better than anybody as long as it's true. And over a course of time, I'll make mistakes and you'll write badly and I'm okay with that. But I'm not okay when it is fake. I mean, I watch CNN — it's so much anger and hatred and just the hatred. I don't watch it anymore because it's very good — he's saying no. It's okay, Jim. It's okay, Jim. You'll have your chance. But I watch others too. You're not the only one, so don't feel badly.

But I think it should be straight. I think it should be — I think it would be, frankly, more interesting. I know how good everybody's ratings are right now, but I think that actually would be — I think that it would actually be better.

People — I mean, you have a lower approval rate than Congress. I think that's right. I don't know, Peter, is that one right? Because you know, I think they have lower — I heard, lower than Congress.

But honestly, the public would appreciate it. I'd appreciate it. Again, I don't mind bad stories when it's true. But we have an administration where the Democrats are making it very difficult. I think we're setting a record, or close to a record in the time of approval of a Cabinet. I mean, the numbers are crazy. When I'm looking — some of them had them approved immediately. I'm going forever, and I still have a lot of people that we're waiting for.

And that's all they're doing, is delaying. And you look at Schumer and the mess that he's got over there, and they have nothing going. The only thing they can do is delay. And you know, I think they'd be better served by approving and making sure that they're happy and everybody is good. And sometimes, I mean — I know President Obama lost three or four, and you lose them on the way. And that's okay. That's fine.

But I think they would be much better served, Jon, if they just went through the process quickly. This is pure delay tactics. And they say it, and everybody understands it.

Yeah, go ahead, Jim.

Q The first part of my question on contacts. Do you definitively say that nobody —

THE PRESIDENT: Well, I had nothing to do with it. I have nothing to do with Russia. I told you, I have no deals there. I have no anything.

Now, when WikiLeaks, which I had nothing to do with, comes out and happens to give — they're not giving classified information. They're giving stuff — what was said at an office about Hillary cheating on the debates — which, by the way, nobody mentions. Nobody mentions that Hillary received the questions to the debates.

Can you imagine — seriously, can you imagine if I received the questions? It would be the electric chair, okay? "He should be put in the electric chair." You would even call for the reinstitution of the death penalty, okay? Maybe not you, Jon.

Yes, we'll do you next, Jim. I'll do you next. Yes?

Q Thank you, Mr. President. I just want to clarify one other thing.

THE PRESIDENT: Sure.

Q Did you direct Mike Flynn to discuss the sanctions with the Russian ambassador?

THE PRESIDENT: No, I didn't. No, I didn't.

Q (Inaudible.) (Off mic.)

THE PRESIDENT: No, I didn't.

Q Did you fire him because (inaudible) —

THE PRESIDENT: Excuse me — no, I fired him because of what he said to Mike Pence, very simple. Mike was doing his job. He was calling countries and his counterparts. So it certainly would have been okay with me if he did it. I would have directed him to do it if I thought he wasn't doing it. I didn't direct him but I would have directed him because that's his job.

And it came out that way — and, in all fairness, I watched Dr. Charles Krauthammer the other night say he was doing his job. And I agreed with him. And since then I've watched many other people say that.

No, I didn't direct him, but I would have directed him if he didn't do it, okay?

Jim.

Q Mr. President, thank you very much. And just for the record, we don't hate you, I don't hate you. If you could pass that along.

THE PRESIDENT: Okay. Well, ask Jeff Zucker how he got his job, okay?

Q If I may follow up on some of the questions that have taken place so far, sir.

THE PRESIDENT: Well, not too many. We do have other people. You do have other people, and your ratings aren't as good as some of the other people that are waiting.

Q They're pretty good right now, actually.

THE PRESIDENT: Okay. Go ahead, Jim.

Q If I may ask, sir, you said earlier that WikiLeaks was revealing information about the Hillary Clinton campaign during the election cycle. You welcomed that at one point.

THE PRESIDENT: I was okay with it.

Q You said you loved WikiLeaks. At another campaign press conference you called on the Russians to find the missing 30,000 emails. I'm wondering, sir, if you —

THE PRESIDENT: Well, she was actually missing 33,000, and then that got extended with a whole pile after that, but that's okay.

Q Maybe my numbers are off a little bit too.

THE PRESIDENT: No, no, but I did say 30,000, but it was actually higher than that.

Q If I may ask you, sir, it sounds as though you do not have much credibility here when it comes to leaking if that is something that you encouraged in the campaign.

THE PRESIDENT: Okay, fair question. Ready?

Q So if I may ask you that — if I may ask a follow-up —

THE PRESIDENT: No, no, but are you — let me do one at a time. Do you mind?

Q Yes, sir.

THE PRESIDENT: All right. So in one case you're talking about highly classified information. In the other case you're talking about John Podesta saying bad things about the boss. I will say this: If John Podesta said that about me and he was working for me, I would have fired him so fast your head would have spun. He said terrible things about her. But it wasn't classified information.

But in one case you're talking about classified. Regardless, if you look at the RNC, we had a very strong — at my suggestion — and I give Reince great credit for this — at my suggestion, because I know something about this world, I said I want a very strong defensive mechanism. I don't want to be hacked. And we did that, and you have seen that they tried to hack us and they failed.

The DNC did not do that. And if they did it, they could not have been hacked. But they were hacked, and terrible things came. And the only thing that I do think is unfair is some of the things were so — they were — when I heard some of those things, I said — I picked up the papers the next morning, I said, oh, this is going to front page. It wasn't even in the papers.

Again, if I had that happen to me, it would be the biggest story in the history of publishing or the head of newspapers. I would have been the headline in every newspaper.

I mean, think of it. They gave her the questions for the debate, and she should have reported herself. Why didn't Hillary Clinton announce that, "I'm sorry, but I have been given the questions to a debate or a town hall, and I feel that it's inappropriate, and I want to turn in CNN for not doing a good job"?

Q And if I may follow up on that, just something that Jonathan Karl was asking you about — you said that the leaks are real, but the news is fake. I guess I don't understand. It seems that there is a disconnect there. If the information coming from those leaks is real, then how can the stories be fake?

THE PRESIDENT: Well, the reporting is fake. Look, look —

Q And if I may ask — I just want to ask one other question.

THE PRESIDENT: Jim, you know what it is? Here's the thing. The public isn't — they read newspapers, they see television, they watch. They don't know if it's true or false because they're not involved. I'm involved. I've been involved with this stuff all my life. But I'm involved. So I know when you're telling the truth or when you're not.

I just see many, many untruthful things. And I tell you what else I see. I see tone. You know the word "tone." The tone is such hatred. I'm really not a bad person, by the way. No, but the tone is such — I do get good ratings, you have to admit that. The tone is such hatred.

I watched this morning a couple of the networks, and I have to say "Fox & Friends" in the morning, they're very honorable people. They're very — not because they're good, because they hit me also when I do something wrong. But they have the most honest morning show. That's all I can say. It's the most honest. But the tone, Jim. If you look — the hatred. I mean, sometimes — sometimes somebody gets —

Q (Off mic.)

THE PRESIDENT: Well, you look at your show that goes on at 10 o'clock in the evening. You just take a look at that show. That is a constant hit. The panel is almost always exclusive anti-Trump. The good news is he doesn't have good ratings. But the panel is almost exclusive anti-Trump. And the hatred and venom coming from his mouth, the hatred coming from other people on your network.

Now, I will say this. I watch it. I see it. I'm amazed by it. And I just think you'd be a lot better off — I honestly do. The public gets it, you know. Look, when I go to rallies, they turn around, they start screaming at CNN. They want to throw their placards at CNN.

I think you would do much better by being different. But you just take a look. Take a look at some of your shows in the morning and the evening. If a guest comes out and says something positive about me, it's brutal.

Now, they'll take this news conference. I'm actually having a very good time, okay? But they'll take this news conference — don't forget that's the way I won. Remember, I used to give you a news conference every time I made a speech, which was like every day.

Q (Off mic.)

THE PRESIDENT: No, that's how I won. I won with news conferences and probably speeches. I certainly didn't win by people listening to you people, that's for sure.

But I am having a good time. Tomorrow they will say, Donald Trump rants and raves at the press. I'm not ranting and raving. I'm just telling you, you're dishonest people. But — but I'm not ranting and raving. I love this. I'm having a good time doing it. But tomorrow the headlines are going to be: Donald Trump Rants and Raves. I'm not ranting and raving.

Q If I may just —

THE PRESIDENT: Go ahead.

Q One more follow-up because —

THE PRESIDENT: Should I let him have a little bit more? What do you think, Peter?

Q Just because of this —

THE PRESIDENT: Peter, should I have let him have a little bit more? Sit down. Sit down.

Q Just because of the attack —

THE PRESIDENT: We'll get it.

Q Just because of the attack of fake news and attacking our network, I just want to ask you, sir —

THE PRESIDENT: I'm changing it from fake news, though.

Q Doesn't that undermine —

THE PRESIDENT: Very fake news now. (Laughter.)

Q But aren't you —

THE PRESIDENT: Yes, go ahead.

Q Real news, Mr. President. Real news.

THE PRESIDENT: And you're not related to our new —

Q I am not related, sir, no. (Laughter.) I do like the sound of Secretary Acosta, I must say.

THE PRESIDENT: I looked — you know, I looked at that name. I said, wait a minute, is there any relation there? Alex Acosta.

Q I'm sure you checked that out, sir.

THE PRESIDENT: No, I checked it. I said — they said, no, sir. I said, do me a favor, go back and check the family tree.

Q But aren't you concerned, sir, that you are undermining the people's faith in the First Amendment freedom of the press, the press in this country when you call stories you don't like "fake news"? Why not just say it's a story I don't like?

THE PRESIDENT: I do that.

Q When you call it fake news, you're undermining confidence —

THE PRESIDENT: No, I do that. No, no, I do that.

Q — in our news media.

THE PRESIDENT: Here's the thing.

Q Isn't that important?

THE PRESIDENT: Okay, I understand — and you're right about that except this. See, I know when I should get good and when I should get bad. And sometimes I'll say, wow, that's going to be a great story, and I'll get killed. I know what's good and bad. I'd be a pretty good reporter — not as good as you. But I know what's good. I know what's bad.

And when they change it and make it really bad — something that should be positive. Sometimes something that should be very positive, they'll make okay. They'll even make it negative. So I understand it because I'm there. I know what was said. I know who is saying it. I'm there. So it's very important to me.

Look, I want to see an honest press. When I started off today by saying that it's so important to the public to get an honest press. The press — the public doesn't believe you people anymore. Now, maybe I had something to do with that, I don't know. But they don't believe you.

If you were straight and really told it like it is, as Howard Cosell used to say, right? Of course, he had some questions also. But if you were straight, I would be your biggest booster, I would be your biggest fan in the world — including bad stories about me. But if you go — as an example, you're CNN — I mean, it's story after story after story is bad. I won. I won. And the other thing: Chaos. There's zero chaos. We are running — this is a fine-tuned machine. And Reince happens to be doing a good job. But half of his job is putting out lies by the press.

I said to him yesterday, this whole Russia scam that you guys are building so that you don't talk about the real subject, which is illegal leaks. But I watched him yesterday working so hard to try and get that story proper. And I'm saying, here's my Chief of Staff, a really good guy, did a phenomenal job at RNC. I mean, we won the election, right? We won the presidency. We got some senators. We got some — all over the country, you take a look, he's done a great job.

And I said to myself, you know — and I said to somebody that was in the room — I said, you take a look at Reince, he's working so hard just putting out fires that are fake fires. They're fake. They're not true. And isn't that a shame, because he'd rather be working on health care. He'd rather be working on tax reform, Jim. I mean that. I would be your biggest fan in the world if you treated me right. I sort of understand there's a certain bias, maybe by Jeff or somebody — for whatever reason. And I understand that. But you've got to be at least a little bit fair. And that's why the public sees it — they see it. They see it's not fair. You take a look at some of your shows and you see the bias and the hatred. And the public is smart. They understand it.

Okay, yeah, go ahead.

Q We have no doubt that your latest story is (inaudible). But for those who believe that there is something to it, is there anything that you have learned over these last few weeks that you might be able to reveal that might ease their concerns that this isn't fake news? And secondly —

THE PRESIDENT: I think they don't believe it. I don't think the public would. That's why the Rasmussen poll just has me through the roof. I don't think they believe it. Well, I guess one of the reasons I'm here today is to tell you the whole Russian thing — that's a ruse. That's a ruse. And, by the way, it would be great if we could get along with Russia, just so you understand that. Now, tomorrow you'll say, Donald Trump wants to get along with Russia, this is terrible. It's not terrible — it's good.

We had Hillary Clinton try and do a reset. We had Hillary Clinton give Russia 20 percent of the uranium in our country. You know what uranium is, right? It's this thing called nuclear weapons and other things. Like, lots of things are done with uranium, including some bad things. Nobody talks about that. I didn't do anything for Russia. I've done nothing for Russia. Hillary Clinton gave them 20 percent of our uranium. Hillary Clinton did a reset, remember, with the stupid plastic button that made us all look like a bunch of jerks? Here, take a look. He looked at her like, what the hell is she doing with that cheap plastic button? Hillary Clinton — that was a reset. Remember? It said "reset."

Now, if I do that, oh, I'm a bad guy. If we could get along with Russia, that's a positive thing. We have a very talented man, Rex Tillerson, who is going to be meeting with them shortly. And I told him, I said, I know politically it's probably not good for me. Hey, the greatest thing I could do is shoot that ship that's 30 miles offshore right out of the water. Everyone in this country is going to say, oh, it's so great. That's not great. That's not great. I would love to be able to get along with Russia.

Now, you've had a lot of Presidents that haven't taken that tact. Look where we are now. Look where we are now. So, if I can — now, I love to negotiate things. I do it really well and all that stuff, but it's possible I won't be able to get along with Putin. Maybe it is. But I want to just tell you, the false reporting by the media, by you people — the false, horrible, fake reporting makes it much harder to make a deal with Russia. And probably Putin said, you know — he's sitting behind his desk and he's saying, you know, I see what's going on in the United States, I follow it closely; it's got to be impossible for President Trump to ever get along with Russia because of all the pressure he's got with this fake story. Okay? And that's a shame. Because if we could get along with Russia — and, by the way, China and Japan and everyone — if we could get along, it would be a positive thing, not a negative thing.

Q Tax reform —

Q Mr. President, since you —

THE PRESIDENT: Tax reform is going to happen fairly quickly. We're doing Obamacare — we're in final stages. We should be submitting the initial plan in March, early March, I would say. And we have to, as you know, statutorily and for reasons of budget, we have to go first. It's not like — frankly, the tax would be easier, in my opinion, but for statutory reasons and for budgetary reasons, we have to submit the health care sooner. So we'll be submitting health care sometime in early March, mid-March. And after that, we're going to come up — and we're doing very well on tax reform.

Yes.

Q Mr. President, you mentioned Russia. Let's talk about some serious issues that have come up in the last week that you have had to deal with as President of the United States.

THE PRESIDENT: Okay.

Q You mentioned the vessel, the spy vessel, off the coast of the United States.

THE PRESIDENT: Not good.

Q There was a ballistic missile test that many interpreted as a violation —

THE PRESIDENT: Not good.

Q — of the agreement between the two countries. And a Russian plane buzzed a U.S. destroyer.

THE PRESIDENT: Not good.

Q I listened to you during the campaign —

THE PRESIDENT: Excuse me, excuse me, when did it happen? It happened when — if you were Putin right now, you would say, hey, we're back to the old games with the United States. There's no way Trump can ever do a deal with us because the — you have to understand, if I was just brutal on Russia right now, just brutal, people would say, you would say, oh, isn't that wonderful. But I know you well enough. Then you would say, oh, he was too tough, he shouldn't have done that. Look, of all —

Q I'm just trying to find out your orientation to those —

THE PRESIDENT: Wait a minute. Wait, wait. Excuse me just one second.

Q I'm just trying to find out what you're doing to do about them, Mr. President.

THE PRESIDENT: All of those things that you mentioned are very recent, because probably Putin assumes that he's not going to be able to make a deal with me because it's politically not popular for me to make a deal. So Hillary Clinton tries to reset, it failed. They all tried. But I'm different than those people.

Go ahead.

Q How are you interpreting those moves? And what do you intend to do about them?

THE PRESIDENT: Just the way I said it.

Q Have you given Rex Tillerson any advice or counsel on how to deal?

THE PRESIDENT: I have. I have. And I'm so beautifully represented. I'm so honored that the Senate approved him. He's going to be fantastic.

Yes, I think that I've already —

Q Is Putin testing you, do you believe, sir?

THE PRESIDENT: No, I don't think so. I think Putin probably assumes that he can't make a deal with me anymore because politically it would be unpopular for a politician to make a deal. I can't believe I'm saying I'm a politician, but I guess that's what I am now. Because, look, it would be much easier for me to be tough on Russia, but then we're not going to make a deal.

Now, I don't know that we're going to make a deal. I don't know. We might, we might not. But it would be much easier for me to be so tough — the tougher I am on Russia, the better. But you know what, I want to do the right thing for the American people. And to be honest, secondarily, I want to do the right thing for the world.

If Russia and the United States actually got together and got along — and don't forget, we're a very powerful nuclear country and so are they. There's no upside. We're a very powerful nuclear country and so are they. I've been briefed. And I can tell you, one thing about a briefing that we're allowed to say because anybody that ever read the most basic book can say it: Nuclear holocaust would be like no other. They're a very powerful nuclear country and so are we.

If we have a good relationship with Russia, believe me, that's a good thing, not a bad thing.

Q So when you say they're not good, do you mean that they are —

THE PRESIDENT: Who did I say is not good?

Q No, when I read off the three things that have recently happened and each one of them you said they're not good.

THE PRESIDENT: No, it's not good, but they happened.

Q But do they damage the relationship? Do they undermine this country's ability to work with Russia?

THE PRESIDENT: They all happened recently, and I understand what they're doing, because they're doing the same thing. Now, again, maybe I'm not going to be able to do a deal with Russia, but at least I will have tried. And if I don't, does anybody really think that Hillary Clinton would be tougher on Russia than Donald Trump? Does anybody in this room really believe that? Okay.

But I tell you one thing: She tried to make a deal. She had the reset. She gave all the valuable uranium away. She did other things. You know, they say I'm close to Russia. Hillary Clinton gave away 20 percent of the uranium in the United States. She's close to Russia. I gave — you know what I gave to Russia? You know what I gave? Nothing.

Q Can we conclude there will be no response to these particular provocations?

THE PRESIDENT: I'm not going to tell you anything about what response I do. I don't talk about military response. I don't say I'm going into Mosul in four months. "We are going to attack Mosul in four months." Then three months later: "We are going to attack Mosul in one month." "Next week, we are going to attack Mosul." In the meantime, Mosul is very, very difficult. Do you know why? Because I don't talk about military, and I don't talk about certain other things. You're going to be surprised to hear that. And, by the way, my whole campaign, I'd say that. So I don't have to tell you —

Q There will be a response?

THE PRESIDENT: I don't want to be one of these guys that say, "Yes, here's what we're going to do." I don't have to do that.

Q There will be a — in other words, there will be a response, Mr. President?

THE PRESIDENT: I don't have to tell you what I'm going to do in North Korea. Wait a minute. I don't have to tell you what I'm going to do in North Korea. And I don't have to tell you what I'm going to do with Iran. You know why? Because they shouldn't know. And eventually you guys are going to get tired of asking that question. So when you ask me, what am I going to do with the ship — the Russian ship, as an example — I'm not going to tell you. But hopefully, I won't have to do anything. But I'm not going to tell you. Okay.

Q Thanks.

Q Can I just ask you — thank you very much, Mr. President — the Trump —

THE PRESIDENT: Where are you from?

Q BBC.

THE PRESIDENT: Okay. Here's another beauty.

Q That's a good line. Impartial, free, and fair.

THE PRESIDENT: Yeah, sure.

Q Mr. President —

THE PRESIDENT: Just like CNN, right?

Q Mr. President, on the travel ban — we could banter back and forth. On the travel ban, would you accept that that was a good example of the smooth running of government, that fine-tuned —

THE PRESIDENT: Yeah, I do. I do. And let me tell you about the travel —

Q Were there any mistakes in that?

THE PRESIDENT: Wait, wait, wait. I know who you are. Just wait. Let me tell you about the travel ban. We had a very smooth rollout of the travel ban, but we had a bad court. We got a bad decision. We had a court that's been overturned — again, maybe wrong, but I think it's 80 percent of the time. A lot. We had a bad decision. We're going to keep going with that decision. We're going to put in a new executive order next week sometime. But we had a bad decision. That's the only thing that was wrong with the travel ban.

You had Delta with a massive problem with their computer system at the airports. You had some people that were put out there, brought by very nice buses, and they were put out at various locations. Despite that, the only problem that we had is we had a bad court. We had a court that gave us what I consider to be, with great respect, a very bad decision. Very bad for the safety and security of our country. The rollout was perfect.

Now, what I wanted to do was do the exact same executive order but said one thing — and I said this to my people: Give them a one-month period of time. But General Kelly, now Secretary Kelly, said, if you do that, all these people will come in, in the month — the bad ones. You do agree, there are bad people out there, right? They're not everybody that's like you. You have some bad people out there.

So Kelly said, you can't do that. And he was right. As soon as he said it, I said, wow, never thought of it. I said, how about one week? He said, no good. You got to do it immediately, because if you do it immediately, they don't have time to come in. Now, nobody ever reports that, but that's why we did it quickly.

Now, if would have done it a month, everything would have been perfect. The problems is we would have wasted a lot of time, and maybe a lot of lives, because a lot of bad people would have come into our country.

Now, in the meantime, we've vetting very, very strongly. Very, very strongly. But we need help, and we need help by getting that executive order passed.

Q Just a brief follow-up. And if it's so urgent, why not introduce —

THE PRESIDENT: Yes, go ahead.

Q Thank you. I just was hoping that we could get a yes- or-no answer on one of these questions involving Russia. Can you say whether you are aware that anyone who advised your campaign had contacts with Russia during the course of the election?

THE PRESIDENT: Well, I told you, General Flynn obviously was dealing. So that's one person. But he was dealing — as he should have been —

Q During the election?

THE PRESIDENT: No, no, nobody that I know of.

Q So you're not aware of any contacts during the course of the election?

THE PRESIDENT: Look, look, how many times do I have to answer this question?

Q Can you just say yes or no on it?

THE PRESIDENT: Russia is a ruse. Yeah, I know you have to get up and ask a question, so important. Russia is a ruse. I have nothing to do with Russia, haven't made a phone call to Russia in years. Don't speak to people from Russia. Not that I wouldn't, I just have nobody to speak to. I spoke to Putin twice. He called me on the election — I told you this — and he called me on the inauguration, and a few days ago. We had a very good talk, especially the second one — lasted for a pretty long period of time. I'm sure you probably get it because it was classified, so I'm sure everybody in this room perhaps has it. But we had a very, very good talk. I have nothing to do with Russia. To the best of my knowledge, no person that I deal with does.

Now, Manafort has totally denied it. He denied it. Now, people knew that he was a consultant over in that part of the world for a while, but not for Russia. I think he represented Ukraine or people having to do with Ukraine, or people that — whoever. But people knew that. Everybody knew that.

Q But in his capacity as your campaign manager, was he in touch with Russian officials during the election?

THE PRESIDENT: I have — you know what, he said no. I can only tell you what he — now, he was replaced long before the election. You know that, right? He was replaced long before the election. When all of this stuff started coming out, it came out during the election. But Paul Manafort, who's a good man also, by the way — Paul Manafort was replaced long before the election took place. He was only there for a short period of time.

How much longer should we stay here, folks? Five more minutes, is that okay? Five?

Q Mr. President, on national security —

THE PRESIDENT: Wait, let's see, who's — I want to find a friendly reporter. Are you a friendly reporter? Watch how friendly he is. Wait, wait — watch how friendly he is. Go ahead. Go ahead.

Q So, first of all, my name is (inaudible) from (inaudible) Magazine. And (inaudible). I haven't seen anybody in my community accuse either yourself or any of the — anyone on your staff of being anti-Semitic. We have an understanding of (inaudible).

THE PRESIDENT: Thank you.

Q However, what we are concerned about, and what we haven't really heard be addressed is an uptick in anti-Semitism and how the government is planning to take care of it. There have been reports out that 48 bomb threats have been made against Jewish centers all across the country in the last couple of weeks. There are people who are committing anti-Semitic acts or threatening to —

THE PRESIDENT: You see, he said he was going to ask a very simple, easy question. And it's not. It's not. Not a simple question, not a fair question. Okay, sit down. I understand the rest of your question.

So here's the story, folks. Number one, I am the least anti-Semitic person that you've ever seen in your entire life. Number two, racism — the least racist person. In fact, we did very well relative to other people running as a Republican.

Q (Inaudible.)

THE PRESIDENT: Quiet, quiet, quiet. See, he lied about — he was going to get up and ask a very straight, simple question. So you know, welcome to the world of the media. But let me just tell you something — that I hate the charge. I find it repulsive. I hate even the question because people that know me — and you heard the Prime Minister, you heard Netanyahu yesterday — did you hear him, Bibi? He said, I've known Donald Trump for a long time, and then he said, forget it.

So you should take that, instead of having to get up and ask a very insulting question like that.

Yeah, go ahead. Go ahead.

Q Thank you. I'm Lisa from the PBS —

THE PRESIDENT: See, it just shows you about the press, but that's the way the press is.

Q Thank you, Mr. President. Lisa Desjardins from the PBS Newshour.

THE PRESIDENT: Good.

Q On national security and immigration, can you give us more details on the executive order you planned for next week, even its broad outlines? Will it be focused on specific countries?

THE PRESIDENT: It's a very fair question.

Q And in addition, on the DACA program for immigration, what is your plan? Do you plan to continue that program or to end it?

THE PRESIDENT: We're going to show great heart. DACA is a very, very difficult subject for me, I will tell you. To me, it's one of the most difficult subjects I have, because you have these incredible kids, in many cases — not in all cases. In some of the cases they're having DACA and they're gang members and they're drug dealers too. But you have some absolutely incredible kids — I would say mostly — they were brought here in such a way — it's a very, very tough subject.

We are going to deal with DACA with heart. I have to deal with a lot of politicians, don't forget, and I have to convince them that what I'm saying is right. And I appreciate your understanding on that.

But the DACA situation is a very, very — it's a very difficult thing for me. Because, you know, I love these kids. I love kids. I have kids and grandkids. And I find it very, very hard doing what the law says exactly to do. And you know, the law is rough. I'm not talking about new laws. I'm talking the existing law is very rough. It's very, very rough.

As far as the new order, the new order is going to be very much tailored to what I consider to be a very bad decision, but we can tailor the order to that decision and get just about everything, in some ways more. But we're tailoring it now to the decision. We have some of the best lawyers in the country working on it. And the new executive order is being tailored to the decision we got down from the court. Okay?

Q Mr. President, Melania Trump announced the reopening of the White House Visitors Office.

THE PRESIDENT: Yes.

Q And she does a lot of great work for the country as well. Can you tell us a little bit about what First Lady Melania Trump does for the country? And there is a unique level of interest in your administration, so by opening the White House Visitors Office, what does that mean to you?

THE PRESIDENT: Now, that's what I call a nice question. That is very nice. Who are you with?

Q (Inaudible.)

THE PRESIDENT: Good. I'm going to start watching. Thank you very much.

Melania is terrific. She was here last night. We had dinner with Senator Rubio and his wife, who is, by the way, lovely. And we had a really good discussion about Cuba because we have very similar views on Cuba. And Cuba was very good to me in the Florida election as you know, the Cuban people, Americans. And I think that Melania is going to be outstanding. That's right, she just opened up the Visitors Center — in other words, touring of the White House.

She, like others that she's working with, feels very, very strongly about women's issues, women's difficulties, very, very strongly. And she's a very, very strong advocate. I think she's a great representative for this country. And a funny thing happens because she gets so unfairly maligned. The things they say — I've known her for a long time. She was a very successful person. She was a very successful model. She did really well. She would go home at night and didn't even want to go out with people. She was a very private person. She was always the highest quality that you'll ever find. And the things they say — and I've known her for a long time — the things they say are so unfair. And actually, she's been apologized to, as you know, by various media because they said things that were lies.

I'd just tell you this: I think she's going to be a fantastic First Lady. She's going to be a tremendous representative of women and of the people. And helping her and working with her will be Ivanka, who is a fabulous person and a fabulous, fabulous woman. And they're not doing this for money. They're not doing this for pay. They're doing this because they feel it, both of them. And Melania goes back and forth, and after Barron finishes school — because it's hard to take a child out of school with a few months left — she and Barron will be moving over to the White House. Thank you. That's a very nice question.

Go ahead.

Q Mr. President.

THE PRESIDENT: Yes. Oh, this is going to be a bad question but that's okay.

Q No, it's not going to be a bad question.

THE PRESIDENT: Good, because I enjoy watching you on television.

Q Well, thank you so much. Mr. President, I need to find out from you — you said something as it relates to inner cities. That was one of your platforms during your campaign.

THE PRESIDENT: Fix the inner cities, yes.

Q Fixing the inner cities. What will be that fix and your urban agenda, as well as your HBCU executive order that's coming out this afternoon? See, it wasn't bad, was it?

THE PRESIDENT: That was very professional and very good.

Q I'm very professional.

THE PRESIDENT: We'll be announcing the order in a little while, and I'd rather let the order speak for itself. But it will be something I think that will be very good for everybody concerned. But we'll talk to you about that after we do the announcement.

As far as the inner cities, as you know, I was very strong on the inner cities during the campaign. I think it's probably what got me a much higher percentage of the African American vote than a lot of people thought I was going to get. We did much higher than people thought I was going to get and I was honored by that, including the Hispanic vote, which was also much higher. And, by the way, if I might add, including the women's vote, which was much higher than people thought I was going to get.

So we are going to be working very hard on the inner cities having to do with education, having to do with crime. We're going to try and fix as quickly as possible — you know it takes a long time. It's taken 100 years or more for some of these places to evolve, and they evolved many of them very badly.

But we're going to be working very hard on health and health care; very, very hard on education. And also, we're going to working in a stringent way, and a very good way, on crime. You go to some of these inner city places, and it's so sad when you look at the crime. You have people — and I've seen this, and I've sort of witnessed it. In fact, in two cases, I have actually witnessed it. They lock themselves into apartments, petrified to even leave, in the middle of the day. They're living in hell. We can't let that happen. So we're going to be very, very strong.

It's a great question, and it's a very difficult situation, because it's been many, many years. It's been festering for many, many years. But we have places in this country that we have to fix. We have to help African American people that, for the most part are stuck there — Hispanic American people. We have Hispanic American people that are in the inner cities, and they're living in hell.

I mean, you look at the numbers in Chicago. There are two Chicagos, as you know. There's one Chicago that's incredible, luxurious and all, and safe. There's another Chicago that's worse than almost any of the places in the Middle East that we talk about, and that you talk about every night on the newscasts. So we're going to do a lot of work on the inner cities. I have great people lined up to help with the inner cities.

Q Well, when you say — when you say the inner cities, are you going to include the CBC, Mr. President, in your conversations with your urban agenda, your inner city agenda, as well as your —

THE PRESIDENT: Am I going include who?

Q Are you going to include the Congressional Black Caucus and the Congressional Hispanic Caucus, as well as —

THE PRESIDENT: Well, I would. I tell you what, do you want to set up the meeting? Do you want to set up the meeting?

Q No, no, no.

THE PRESIDENT: Are they friends of yours?

Q I'm just a reporter.

THE PRESIDENT: No, go ahead, set up the meeting.

Q I know some of them, but I'm sure they're watching right now.

THE PRESIDENT: Let's go set up a meeting. I would love to meet with the Black Caucus. I think it's great — the Congressional Black Caucus. I think it's great. I actually thought I had a meeting with Congressman Cummings, and he was all excited, and then he said, oh, I can't move, it might be bad for me politically, I can't have that meeting. I was all set to have the meeting. You know, we called him and called him, and he was all set. I spoke to him on the phone. Very nice guy.

Q I hear he wanted that meeting with you as well.

THE PRESIDENT: He wanted it. But we called, called, called, called — they can't make a meeting with him. Every day, I walked in, I said, I would like to meet with him. Because I do want to solve the problem. But he probably was told by Schumer or somebody like that — some other lightweight — he was probably told — he was probably told, don't meet with Trump, it's bad politics. And that's part of the problem of this country.

Okay, one more. Go ahead.

Q Yes, Mr. President, two questions —

THE PRESIDENT: No, no. One question. Two, we can't handle. This room can't handle two. Go ahead, give me the better of your two.

Q (Inaudible) it's not about your personality or your beliefs. We're talking about (inaudible) around the country, some of it by supporters in your name. What do you —

THE PRESIDENT: And some of it — and can I be honest with you? And this has to do with racism and horrible things that are put up. Some of it written by our opponents. You do know that. Do you understand that? You don't think anybody would do a thing like that. Some of the signs you'll see are not put up by the people that love or like Donald Trump, they're put up by the other side, and you think it's like playing it straight. No. But you have some of those signs, and some of that anger is caused by the other side. They'll do signs and they'll do drawings that are inappropriate. It won't be my people. It will be the people on the other side to anger people like you. Okay.

Go ahead.

Q You are the President now. What are you going to do about it?

THE PRESIDENT: Who is that? Where is that? Oh, stand up. You can —

Q What are you going to do about the tensions that have been discussed?

THE PRESIDENT: Oh, I'm working on it. No, I'm working on it very hard.

Q Are you going to give a speech?

THE PRESIDENT: No, no, look. Hey, just so you understand, we had a totally divided country for eight years, and long before that, in all fairness to President Obama. Long before President Obama, we have had a very divided. I didn't come along and divide this country. This country was seriously divided before I got here.

We're going to work on it very hard. One of the questions that was asked — I thought it was a very good question — was about the inner cities. I mean, that's part of it. But we're going to work on education. We're going to work on lack — you know, we're going to stop — we're going to try and stop the crime. We have great law enforcement officials. We're going to try and stop crime. We're not going to try and stop, we're going to stop crime.

But it's very important to me. But this isn't Donald Trump that divided a nation. We went eight years with President Obama, and we went many years before President Obama. We lived in a divided nation. And I am going to try — I will do everything within my power to fix that.

I want to thank everybody very much. It's a great honor to be with you. Thank you. Thank you very much. (Applause.)

Trump Remarks on African American History Month

This is an annotated transcript of remarks by President Trump on Feb. 1 in the Roosevelt Room at the White House.

THE PRESIDENT: Hello, everybody. These are a lot of my friends, but you have been so helpful. And we did well. The election, it came out really well. Next time we'll triple it up or quadruple it, right? We want to get over 51, right? At least 51.

Well, this is Black History Month, so this is our little breakfast, our little get-together. Hi, Lynne, how are you?

MS. PATTON: Hi, how are you?

THE PRESIDENT: Nice to see you. And just a few notes. During this month, we honor the tremendous history of the African Americans throughout our country — throughout the world, if you really think about it, right? And their story is one of unimaginable sacrifice, hard work and faith in America.

I've gotten a real glimpse — during the campaign, I'd go around with Ben to a lot of different places that I wasn't so familiar with. They're incredible people. And I want to thank Ben Carson, who's going to be heading up HUD. It's a big job, and it's a job that's not only housing, it's mind and spirit, right, Ben? And you understand that. Nobody is going to be better than Ben.

Last month, we celebrated the life of the Reverend Martin Luther King, Jr., whose incredible example is unique in American history. You read all about Dr. Martin Luther King a week ago when somebody said I took the statue out of my office, and it turned out that that was fake news. (Laughter.) It was fake news. The statue is cherished. It's one of the favorite things in the — and we have some good ones. We have Lincoln and we have Jefferson and we have Dr. Martin Luther King, and we have — but they said the statue, the bust of Dr. Martin Luther King was taken out of the office. And it was never even touched. So I think it was a disgrace, but that's the way the press is. Very unfortunate.

I am very proud now that we have a museum on the National Mall where people can learn about Reverend King, so many other things. Frederick Douglass is an example of somebody who's done an amazing job and is being recognized more and more, I notice — Harriet Tubman, Rosa Parks, and millions more black Americans who made America what it is today. Big impact.

I am proud to honor this heritage, and we'll be honoring it more and more. The folks at the table in almost all cases have been great friends and supporters. And Darrell — I met Darrell when he was defending me on television. (Laughter.) And the people that were on the other side of the argument didn't have a chance, right? And Paris has done an amazing job in a very hostile CNN community. (Laughter.) He's all by himself — seven people and Paris. So I'll take Paris over the seven. (Laughter.) But I don't watch CNN so I don't get to see you as much as I want to. (Laughter.) I don't like watching fake news.

PARTICIPANT: None of us watch it either anymore.

THE PRESIDENT: But Fox has treated me very nice — wherever Fox is, thank you.

We're going to need better schools, and we need them soon. We need more jobs, we need better wages — a lot better wages. We're going to work very hard on the inner city. Ben is going to be doing that big league. It's one of his big things that we're going to be looking at.

We need safer communities, and we're going to do that with law enforcement. We're going to make it safe. We're going to make it much better than it is right now. Right now it's terrible, and I saw you talking about it the other night, Paris, on something else that was really — you did a fantastic job the other night on a very unrelated show. I'm ready to do my part — it's the only time I can see him. I'm ready to do my part, and I will say this: We're going to work together.

This is a great group. This is a group that's been so special to me. You really helped me a lot. If you remember, I wasn't going to do well with the African American community, and after they heard me speaking and talking about the inner city and lots of other things, we ended up getting — I won't go into details, but we ended up getting substantially more than other candidates who had run in the past years. And now, we're going to take that to new levels.

I want to thank my television star over here. (Laughter.) Omarosa is actually a very nice person. Nobody knows that, but — (laughter) — I don't want to destroy her reputation. She is a very good person and she's been helpful right from the beginning of the campaign. And I appreciate it. I really do. Very special.

And so I want to thank everybody for being here. Could we maybe just go around the room and we'll introduce ourselves. And the press can stay for that, and I'm sure they have no questions about last night because it was such a good launch. We have a fantastic, hopefully, new justice of the Supreme Court. And hopefully, that will be — he'll be approved very, very quickly. He's outstanding in every way — academically. He's done almost as well as you did, Darrell, in college. (Laughter.) Not quite, right? But he's a great man and I think he'll be a great, great justice. And he's being very well-received. It was a big evening. Very big evening.

So, Paris, why don't we start with you? Go ahead.

MR. DENNARD: Pleasure to be here, Mr. President. Honor to be here. Paris Dennard. Thurgood Marshall College Fund represents the 47 publically supported historically black colleges and universities, which I know you are very much in support of. So it's a pleasure to be here, sir.

THE PRESIDENT: Well, I'm glad you're in support of me because I'd be all — I'd be in the wilderness without you guys. You are so effective. I appreciate it.

MR. DENNARD: Thank you.

THE PRESIDENT: Thank you.

MR. CLEVELAND: Bill Cleveland. I'm a retired Capitol police officer, former vice mayor of the city of Alexandria, and substitute teacher in the Alexandria school system. Glad to be here.

THE PRESIDENT: Thank you. Thank you.

MR. MATTHEWS: Bill is also a Vietnam veteran, sir.

THE PRESIDENT: Oh, good.

MR. MATTHEWS: I'm Earl Matthews, sir. I work for you at the Department of Defense. I was sworn in an hour after you were. Also a veteran and a longtime supporter of yours. I've worked for you since late summer. I'm happy to be here.

THE PRESIDENT: Lieutenant Colonel — good job.

MS. SCOTT: I'm Belinda Scott, Darrell's wife. New Spirit Revival Center from Cleveland, Ohio. Pastor of New Spirit. Great amount of support in the African American community where we are. We love the Lord, we love our new President, and we are praying for our President on a regular basis.

THE PRESIDENT: You know, the one thing I didn't understand about Belinda — I thought they were married maybe five or six years, because look how they look so young. (Laughter.) Should you say how many years you've been married?

MS. SCOTT: Thirty-five.

PASTOR SCOTT: We've been together for 38.

MS. SCOTT: Been together for — but in the Lord –(laughter) — 35, yes.

PASTOR SCOTT: Two years under — (inaudible.) (Laughter.)

THE PRESIDENT: That's actually amazing. I wouldn't have known.

MS. SCOTT: But can I say this — I am so grateful that our President gives us that ear to listen to the community — to listen. And people like us are just here to constantly put that message out into the community. And we love you for that. We love you for listening and we thank you for that.

THE PRESIDENT: Thank you. Thank you very much.

PASTOR SCOTT: Darrell Scott, pastor at New Spirit Revival Center and black Trump supporter. (Laughter and applause.) But speaking of the community, let me just say this real quick. Omarosa, I told you I'm going to try to throw it in. I was recently contacted by some of the top gang thugs initiative Chicago for a sit-down. They reached out to me because they associated me with you. They respect you, they believe in what you're doing, and they want to have a sit-down about lowering that body count. So in a couple of weeks, I'm going into Chicago.

THE PRESIDENT: That's a great idea because Chicago is totally out of control.

PASTOR SCOTT: Well, I let him know — I said, we've got to lower that body count. We don't want to talk about anything else — get that body count down. And they agreed. But the principle is they can do it. These are guys straight from the streets — no politicians — straight street guys. But they're going to commit that if they lower that body count, we'll come in and we'll do some social programs. So they're in agreement.

THE PRESIDENT: If they're not going to solve the problem — and what you're doing is the right thing — then we're going to solve the problem for them because we're going to have to do something about Chicago. Because what's happening in Chicago should not be happening in this country.

PASTOR SCOTT: But they want to work with this administration.

THE PRESIDENT: Good.

PASTOR SCOTT: They want to. They reached out — I didn't reach out to them. They reached out to me.

THE PRESIDENT: I understand.

PASTOR SCOTT: They want to work with this administration. They believe in this administration. They didn't believe in the prior administration. They told me this out of their mouth. But they see hope with you.

PRESIDENT TRUMP: I love it.

MR. WILLIAMS: Mr. President, I'm a member of what we call the media, but we try to be fair and objective. (Laughter.) Not all media seems to be the opposition party. There are those that see the good that you're doing. We report it. I'm just honored to have a seat at the table today.

THE PRESIDENT: Thank you. And it is — I mean, a lot of the media is actually the opposition party. They're so biased and really is a disgrace. Some of you are fantastic and fair, but so much of the media is opposition party and knowingly saying incorrect things. So it's a very sad situation. But we seem to be doing well. It's almost like, in the meantime, we won. So maybe they don't have the influence they think, but they really are — they really have to straighten out their act. They're very dishonest people.

James.

PASTOR DAVIS: Pastor James Davis. We've been — Mr. President, we've been a supporter of yours from the beginning alongside Mr. Michael Cohen and Dr. Darrell Scott with the National Diversity Coalition. It helped to bring out a huge number in the black community with respect to the vote. And we're still happy to be in support as we go forward.

THE PRESIDENT: Thank you. You've been great. Thank you, James.

And, Lynne.

MS. PATTON: Hi, Mr. President. Yes, I am, as you know, the former vice president of the wonderful charity that your son founded — Trump Foundation. I've been with your family for about eight years now, right, Jared? And I was an RNC speaker and I will be landing with Dr. Carson at HUD as one of his senior advisors —

THE PRESIDENT: Oh, that's great. You've got a good person.

MS. PATTON: — and Director of the Office of Public Liaison.

THE PRESIDENT: That's great. You did a fantastic job.

MS. PATTON: Thank you.

MR. ROBINSON: Mr. President, my name is Gerard Robinson. I'm a resident fellow at the American Enterprise Institute, and I was proud to be the leader of the education policy team for the Trump transition.

THE PRESIDENT: Thank you.

MR. BELL: Mr. President, good to be with you. I'm Ashley Bell, Gainesville. Chairman Priebus called me out (inaudible) African American outreach for your campaign. I'm glad you support Omarosa, glad to be here, and I'll be wanting to help you out at the State Department.

THE PRESIDENT: Fantastic. Thank you. Thank you very much.

MS. MANIGAULT: Tucker was a star at the inauguration.

MR. DAVIS: I'm Tucker Davis. I ran your campaign in West Virginia, working for you in the —

THE PRESIDENT: We did well in West Virginia. (Laughter.)

MR. DAVIS: Coal miners love you.

THE PRESIDENT: And we love the coal miners. We're going to put them back to work.

MR. DAVIS: Absolutely.

MS. LEVELL: Leah LeVell. I was at the RNC and also at PIC. And I helped launch the video series every week — the midweek message that reached out to millennials and college students and helped launch the college Republican chapter at Howard University.

MS. MANIGAULT: That's Chris LeVell's daughter. We snagged her. (Laughter.)

THE PRESIDENT: Oh, really? Great job.

MS. ALEXANDER: Mr. President, Monica Alexander, executive administrative assistant in the office of public liaison, supporting Omarosa.

PRESIDENT TRUMP: Okay, well, that's nice.

MR. SMITH: Mr. President, Ja'Ron Smith. I'm with the Domestic Policy Council, Andy Bremberg's team, and I'll be focusing on urban affairs and revitalization.

THE PRESIDENT: Fantastic.

MS. MANIGAULT: And Howard graduate. (Laughter.)

THE PRESIDENT: Howard graduate. That's good stuff. Thank you, everybody. Thank you.

President Trump Statement on Immigration

The White House issued the following statement on Jan. 29.

President Donald J. Trump Statement Regarding Recent Executive Order Concerning Extreme Vetting:

America is a proud nation of immigrants and we will continue to show compassion to those fleeing oppression, but we will do so while protecting our own citizens and border. America has always been the land of the free and home of the brave. We will keep it free and keep it safe, as the media knows, but refuses to say.

My policy is similar to what President Obama did in 2011 when he banned visas for refugees from Iraq for six months. The seven countries named in the Executive Order are the same countries previously identified by the Obama administration as sources of terror.

To be clear, this is not a Muslim ban, as the media is falsely reporting. This is not about religion – this is about terror and keeping our country safe. There are over 40 different countries worldwide that are majority Muslim that are not affected by this order.

We will again be issuing visas to all countries once we are sure we have reviewed and implemented the most secure policies over the next 90 days. I have tremendous feeling for the people involved in this horrific humanitarian crisis in Syria. My first priority will always be to protect and serve our country, but as President I will find ways to help all those who are suffering.

Remarks by President Trump and Vice President Pence at CIA Headquarters

This is an annotated transcript of remarks by President Trump and Vice President Pence at CIA Headquarters in Langley, Virginia, on Jan. 21, 2017.

VICE PRESIDENT PENCE: Thank you to the Acting Director Meroe Park. Thank you for 27 years serving the United States of America here at CIA. (Applause.)

It's a great privilege for me to be with you today and to have the opportunity to introduce at his first event, on his first full day, the new President of the United States, Donald Trump. (Applause.)

As you can imagine, it's deeply humbling for my family and I to find ourselves in this role. I'm grateful to our new President for the opportunity he's given me and the opportunity the American people have given us to serve. But it's especially humbling for me to be before all of you today — men and women of character, who have sacrificed greatly — and to stand before this hallowed wall, this memorial wall, where we remember 117 who paid the ultimate sacrifice for our freedom.

I can assure you this new President and our entire team recognizes and appreciates the sacrifices of all of the men and women of the intelligence community of the United States of America. (Applause.)

I've gotten to know our new President. We traveled a lot together. When the cameras are off and the — lights are off, I'll tell you two things I know for sure. Number one, I've never met anyone more dedicated to the safety and security of the people of the United States of America, or anyone who is a greater strategic thinker about how we accomplish that for this nation. In fact, to understand the life of our new President is — his whole life was strategy. He built an extraordinary success in the private sector, and I know he's going to make America safe again. (Applause.)

And lastly, I can honestly tell you, for all my years serving in the Congress, serving as governor of my home state, traveling cross-country and seeing the connection that he's made to men and women who serve and protect in every capacity in this country, I've never met anyone with a greater heart for those who every day, in diverse ways, protect the people of this nation through their character and their service and their sacrifice.

And so let me say, it is my high honor and distinct privilege to introduce all of you the President of the United States. (Applause.)

PRESIDENT TRUMP: Well, I want to thank everybody. Very, very special people. And it is true, this is my first stop, officially. We're not talking about the balls, or we're not talking about even the speeches — although they did treat me nicely on that speech yesterday. (Laughter.) I always call them the dishonest media, but they treated me nicely. (Laughter.)

But I want to say that there is nobody that feels stronger about the intelligence community and the CIA than Donald Trump. There's nobody. (Applause.)

The wall behind me is very, very special. We've been touring for quite a while, and I'll tell you what — 29? I can't believe it.

AUDIENCE MEMBER: Twenty-eight.

PRESIDENT TRUMP: Oh, 28. We got to reduce it. That's amazing. And we really appreciate what you've done in terms of showing us something very special. And your whole group, these are really special, amazing people. Very, very few people could do the job you people do. And I want to just let you know, I am so behind you. And I know maybe sometimes you haven't gotten the backing that you've wanted, and you're going to get so much backing. Maybe you're going to say, please don't give us so much backing. (Laughter.) Mr. President, please, we don't need that much backing. (Laughter.) But you're going to have that. And I think everybody in this room knows it.

You know, the military and the law enforcement, generally speaking, but all of it — but the military gave us tremendous percentages of votes. We were unbelievably successful in the election with getting the vote of the military. And probably almost everybody in this room voted for me, but I will not ask you to raise your hands if you did. (Laughter.) But I would guarantee a big portion, because we're all on the same wavelength, folks. (Applause.) We're all on the same wavelength, right? He knows. It took Brian about 30 seconds to figure that one out, right, because we know we're on the same wavelength.

But we're going to do great things. We're going to do great things. We've been fighting these wars for longer than any wars we've ever fought. We have not used the real abilities that we have. We've been restrained. We have to get rid of ISIS. Have to get rid of ISIS. We have no choice. (Applause.) Radical Islamic terrorism. And I said it yesterday — it has to be eradicated just off the face of the Earth. This is evil. This is evil. And you know, I can understand the other side. We can all understand the other side. There can be wars between countries, there can be wars. You can understand what happened. This is something nobody can even understand. This is a level of evil that we haven't seen. And you're going to go to it, and you're going to do a phenomenal job. But we're going to end it. It's time. It's time right now to end it.

You have somebody coming on who is extraordinary. For the different positions of "Secretary of This" and "Secretary of That" and all of these great positions, I'd see five, six, seven, eight people. And we had a great transition. We had an amazing team of talent. And, by the way, General Flynn is right over here. Put up your hand. What a good guy. (Applause.) And Reince and my whole group. Reince — you know — they don't care about

Reince. He's like this political guy that turned out to be a superstar, right? We don't have to talk about Reince.

But we did — we had such a tremendous, tremendous success. So when I'm interviewing all of these candidates that Reince and his whole group is putting in front, it went very, very quickly, and, in this case, went so quickly — because I would see six or seven or eight for Secretary of Agriculture, who we just named the other day, Sonny Perdue, former governor of Georgia. Fantastic guy. But I'd see six, seven, eight people for a certain position. Everybody wanted it.

But I met Mike Pompeo, and it was the only guy I met. I didn't want to meet anybody else. I said, cancel everybody else. Cancel. Now, he was approved, essentially, but they're doing little political games with me. He was one of the three. Now, last night, as you know, General Mattis, fantastic guy, and General Kelly got approved. (Applause.) And Mike Pompeo was supposed to be in that group. It was going to be the three of them. Can you imagine all of these guys? People respect — you know, they respect that military sense. All my political people, they're not doing so well. The political people aren't doing so well but you. We're going to get them all through, but some will take a little bit longer than others.

But Mike was literally — I had a group of — what, we had nine different people? Now, I must say, I didn't mind cancelling eight appointments. That wasn't the worst thing in the world. But I met him and I said, he is so good. Number one in his class at West Point.

Now, I know a lot about West Point. I'm a person that very strongly believes in academics. In fact, every time I say I had an uncle who was a great professor at MIT for 35 years who did a fantastic job in so many different ways, academically — was an academic genius — and then they say, is Donald Trump an intellectual? Trust me, I'm like a smart persona. (Laughter.) And I recognized immediately. So he was number one at West Point, and he was also essentially number one at Harvard Law School. And then he decided to go into the military. And he ran for Congress. And everything he's done has been a home run. People like him, but much more importantly to me, everybody respects him. And when I told Paul Ryan that I wanted to do this, I would say he may be the only person that was not totally thrilled — right, Mike? Because he said, I don't want to lose this guy.

But you will be getting a total star. You're going to be getting a total gem. He's a gem. (Applause.) You'll see. You'll see. And many of you know him anyway. But you're going to see. And again, we have some great people going in. But this one is something — is going to be very special, because this is one, if I had to name the most important, this would certainly be perhaps — you know, in certain ways, you could say my most important. You do the job like everybody in this room is capable of doing. And the generals are wonderful, and the fighting is wonderful. But if you give them the right direction, boy, does the fighting become easier. And, boy, do we lose so fewer lives, and win so quickly. And that's what we have to do. We have to start winning again.

You know, when I was young and when I was — of course, I feel young. I feel like I'm 30, 35, 39. (Laughter.) Somebody said, are you young? I said, I think I'm young. You know, I was stopping — when we were in the final month of that campaign, four stops, five stops, seven stops. Speeches, speeches, in front of 25,000, 30,000 people, 15,000, 19,000 from stop to stop. I feel young.

When I was young — and I think we're all sort of young. When I was young, we were always winning things in this country. We'd win with trade. We'd win with wars. At a certain age, I remember hearing from one of my instructors, "The United States has never lost a war." And then, after that, it's like we haven't won anything. We don't win anymore. The old expression, "to the victor belong the spoils" — you remember. I always used to say, keep the oil. I wasn't a fan of Iraq. I didn't want to go into Iraq. But I will tell you, when we were in, we got out wrong. And I always said, in addition to that, keep the oil. Now, I said it for economic reasons. But if you think about it, Mike, if we kept the oil you probably wouldn't have ISIS because that's where they made their money in the first place. So we should have kept the oil. But okay. (Laughter.) Maybe you'll have another chance. But the fact is, should have kept the oil.

I believe that this group is going to be one of the most important groups in this country toward making us safe, toward making us winners again, toward ending all of the problems. We have so many problems that are interrelated that we don't even think of, but interrelated to the kind of havoc and fear that this sick group of people has caused. So I can only say that I am with you 1,000 percent.

And the reason you're my first stop is that, as you know, I have a running war with the media. They are among the most dishonest human beings on Earth. (Laughter and applause.) And they sort of made it sound like I had a feud with the intelligence community. And I just want to let you know, the reason you're the number-one stop is exactly the opposite — exactly. And they understand that, too.

And I was explaining about the numbers. We did a thing yesterday at the speech. Did everybody like the speech? (Applause.) I've been given good reviews. But we had a massive field of people. You saw them. Packed. I get up this morning, I turn on one of the networks, and they show an empty field. I say, wait a minute, I made a speech. I looked out, the field was — it looked like a million, million and a half people. They showed a field where there were practically nobody standing there. And they said, Donald Trump did not draw well. I said, it was almost raining, the rain should have scared them away, but God looked down and he said, we're not going to let it rain on your speech.

In fact, when I first started, I said, oh, no. The first line, I got hit by a couple of drops. And I said, oh, this is too bad, but we'll go right through it. But the truth is that it stopped immediately. It was amazing. And then it became really sunny. And then I walked off and it poured right after I left. It poured. But, you know, we have something that's amazing because we had — it looked — honestly, it looked like a million and a half people. Whatever it was, it was. But it went all the way back to the Washington Monument. And I turn on — and by mistake I get this network, and it showed an empty field. And it said we drew 250,000 people. Now, that's not bad, but it's a lie. We had 250,000 people literally around — you know, in the little bowl that we constructed. That was 250,000 people. The rest of the 20-block area, all the way back to the Washington Monument, was packed. So we caught them, and we caught them in a beauty. And I think they're going to pay a big price.

We had another one yesterday, which was interesting. In the Oval Office there's a beautiful statue of Dr. Martin Luther King. And I also happen to like Churchill, Winston Churchill. I think most of us like Churchill. He doesn't come from our country, but had a lot to do with it. Helped us; real ally. And, as you know, the Churchill statue was taken out — the bust. And as you also probably have read, the Prime Minister is coming over to our country very shortly. And they wanted to know whether or not I'd like it back. I say, absolutely, but in the meantime we have a bust of Churchill.

So a reporter for Time magazine — and I have been on there cover, like, 14 or 15 times. I think we have the all-time record in the history of Time Magazine. Like, if Tom Brady is on the cover, it's one time, because he won the Super Bowl or something, right? (Laughter.) I've been on it for 15 times this year. I don't think that's a record, Mike, that can ever be broken. Do you agree with that? What do you think?

But I will say that they said — it was very interesting — that Donald Trump took down the bust, the statue, of Dr. Martin Luther King. And it was right there. But there was a cameraman that was in front of it. (Laughter.) So Zeke — Zeke from Time Magazine writes a story about I took down. I would never do that because I have great respect for Dr. Martin Luther King. But this is how dishonest the media is.

Now, the big story — the retraction was, like, where? Was it a line? Or do they even bother putting it in? So I only like to say that because I love honesty. I like honest reporting.

I will tell you, final time — although I will say it, when you let in your thousands of other people that have been trying to come in — because I am coming back — we're going to have to get you a larger room. (Applause.) We may have to get you a larger room. You know? And maybe, maybe, it will be built by somebody that knows how to build, and we won't have columns. (Laughter.) You understand that? (Applause.) We get rid of the columns.

No, I just wanted to really say that I love you, I respect you. There's nobody I respect more. You're going to do a fantastic job. And we're going to start winning again, and you're going to be leading the charge.

So thank you all very much. (Applause.) Thank you — you're beautiful. Thank you all very much. Have a good time. I'll be back. I'll be back. Thank you.

President Donald J. Trump Inaugural Address

*This is an annotated transcript of President Donald J. Trump's
inaugural address on Jan. 20, 2017.*

Chief Justice Roberts, President Carter, President Clinton,
President Bush, President Obama, fellow Americans, and people of
the world: thank you.

We, the citizens of America, are now joined in a great national
effort to rebuild our country and to restore its promise for all of our
people.

Together, we will determine the course of America and the world
for many, many years to come.

We will face challenges. We will confront hardships. But we will
get the job done.

Every four years, we gather on these steps to carry out the orderly
and peaceful transfer of power, and we are grateful to President
Obama and First Lady Michelle Obama for their gracious aid
throughout this transition. They have been magnificent. Thank
you.

Today's ceremony, however, has very special meaning. Because
today we are not merely transferring power from one
administration to another, or from one party to another – but we
are transferring power from Washington, D.C. and giving it back
to you, the people.

For too long, a small group in our nation's Capital has reaped the rewards of government while the people have borne the cost.

Washington flourished – but the people did not share in its wealth.

Politicians prospered – but the jobs left, and the factories closed.

The establishment protected itself, but not the citizens of our country.

Their victories have not been your victories; their triumphs have not been your triumphs; and while they celebrated in our nation's Capital, there was little to celebrate for struggling families all across our land.

That all changes – starting right here, and right now, because this moment is your moment: it belongs to you.

It belongs to everyone gathered here today and everyone watching all across America.

This is your day. This is your celebration.

And this, the United States of America, is your country.

What truly matters is not which party controls our government, but whether our government is controlled by the people.

January 20, 2017, will be remembered as the day the people became the rulers of this nation again.

The forgotten men and women of our country will be forgotten no longer.

Everyone is listening to you now.

You came by the tens of millions to become part of a historic movement the likes of which the world has never seen before.

At the center of this movement is a crucial conviction: that a nation exists to serve its citizens.

Americans want great schools for their children, safe neighborhoods for their families, and good jobs for themselves.

These are the just and reasonable demands of righteous people and a righteous public.

But for too many of our citizens, a different reality exists: Mothers and children trapped in poverty in our inner cities; rusted-out factories scattered like tombstones across the landscape of our nation; an education system, flush with cash, but which leaves our young and beautiful students deprived of all knowledge; and the crime and the gangs and the drugs that have stolen too many lives and robbed our country of so much unrealized potential.

This American carnage stops right here and stops right now.

We are one nation – and their pain is our pain. Their dreams are our dreams; and their success will be our success. We share one heart, one home, and one glorious destiny.

The oath of office I take today is an oath of allegiance to all Americans.

For many decades, we've enriched foreign industry at the expense of American industry. Subsidized the armies of other countries while allowing for the very sad depletion of our military. We've defended other nation's borders while refusing to defend our own. And spent trillions and trillions of dollars overseas while America's infrastructure has fallen into disrepair and decay.

We've made other countries rich while the wealth, strength, and confidence of our country has dissipated over the horizon.

One by one, the factories shuttered and left our shores, with not even a thought about the millions and millions of American workers left behind.

The wealth of our middle class has been ripped from their homes and then redistributed all across the world.

But that is the past. And now we are looking only to the future.

We assembled here today are issuing a new decree to be heard in every city, in every foreign capital, and in every hall of power.

From this day forward, a new vision will govern our land.

From this moment on, it's going to be only America First. America First.

Every decision on trade, on taxes, on immigration, on foreign affairs, will be made to benefit American workers and American families.

We must protect our borders from the ravages of other countries making our products, stealing our companies, and destroying our jobs. Protection will lead to great prosperity and strength.

I will fight for you with every breath in my body – and I will never, ever let you down.

America will start winning again, winning like never before.

We will bring back our jobs. We will bring back our borders. We will bring back our wealth. And we will bring back our dreams.

We will build new roads, and highways, and bridges, and airports, and tunnels, and railways all across our wonderful nation.

We will get our people off of welfare and back to work – rebuilding our country with American hands and American labor.

We will follow two simple rules: Buy American and hire American.

We will seek friendship and goodwill with the nations of the world – but we do so with the understanding that it is the right of all nations to put their own interests first.

We do not seek to impose our way of life on anyone, but rather to let it shine as an example — we will shine — for everyone to follow.

We will reinforce old alliances and form new ones – and unite the civilized world against radical Islamic terrorism, which we will eradicate completely from the face of the Earth.

At the bedrock of our politics will be a total allegiance to the United States of America, and through our loyalty to our country, we will rediscover our loyalty to each other.

When you open your heart to patriotism, there is no room for prejudice.

The Bible tells us, "how good and pleasant it is when God's people live together in unity."

We must speak our minds openly, debate our disagreements honestly, but always pursue solidarity.

When America is united, America is totally unstoppable.

There should be no fear – we are protected, and we will always be protected. We will be protected by the great men and women of our military and law enforcement and, most importantly, we will be protected by God.

Finally, we must think big and dream even bigger.

In America, we understand that a nation is only living as long as it is striving.

We will no longer accept politicians who are all talk and no action – constantly complaining but never doing anything about it.

The time for empty talk is over. Now arrives the hour of action.

Do not allow anyone to tell you it cannot be done. No challenge can match the heart and fight and spirit of America.

We will not fail. Our country will thrive and prosper again.

We stand at the birth of a new millennium, ready to unlock the mysteries of space, to free the Earth from the miseries of disease, and to harness the energies, industries and technologies of tomorrow.

A new national pride will stir our souls, lift our sights, and heal our divisions.

It's time to remember that old wisdom our soldiers will never forget: that whether we are black or brown or white, we all bleed the same red blood of patriots. We all enjoy the same glorious freedoms, and we all salute the same great American flag.

And whether a child is born in the urban sprawl of Detroit or the windswept plains of Nebraska, they look up at the same night sky, they fill their heart with the same dreams, and they are infused with the breath of life by the same almighty Creator.

So to all Americans, in every city near and far, small and large, from mountain to mountain, and from ocean to ocean, hear these words: You will never be ignored again.

Your voice, your hopes, and your dreams, will define our American destiny. And your courage and goodness and love will forever guide us along the way.

Together, We will make America strong again.

We will make America wealthy again.

We will make America proud again.

We will make America safe again.

And, yes, together, we will make America great again.

Thank you, God bless you, and God bless America.

Thank you. God bless America.

Trump Rally in Arizona

*President Trump gave a campaign-style rally
in Arizona in August 2017.*

TRUMP: What a crowd.

(APPLAUSE)

TRUMP: And just so you know from the Secret Service, there aren't too many people outside protesting, OK. That I can tell you.

(APPLAUSE)

A lot of people in here, a lot of people pouring right now. They can get them in. Whatever you can do, fire marshals, we'll appreciate it.

TRUMP: And I want to thank our great vice president, Mike Pence, for the introduction.

(APPLAUSE)

As well as my friend Dr. Ben Carson.

(APPLAUSE)

And thank you to a very, very special man, Franklin Graham, Reverend Franklin Graham, for leading us in prayer.

(APPLAUSE)

And thank you too Alveda King, the niece of the great Dr. Martin Luther King.

(APPLAUSE)

It really shows you that America is indeed a nation of faith, we know that.

(APPLAUSE)

Well, I'm thrilled to be back in Phoenix, in the great state of Arizona.

(APPLAUSE)

With so many thousands of hard-working American patriots.

You know I'd love it if the cameras could show this crowd, because it is rather incredible. It is incredible.

(APPLAUSE)

It is incredible.

As everybody here remembers, this was the scene of my first rally speech, right?

The crowds were so big, almost as big as tonight, that the people said right at the beginning, you know, there's something special happening here. And we went to center stage almost from day one in the debates. We love those debates.

(APPLAUSE)

But we went to center stage and we never left, right? All of us, we did it together.

You were there at the start. You've been there every single day since, and I will never forget. Believe me, Arizona, I will never forget.

(APPLAUSE)

And I'm here tonight to send a message: We are fully and totally committed to fighting for our agenda, and we will not stop until the job is done.

(APPLAUSE)

This evening, joined together with friends, we reaffirm our shared customs, traditions and values. We love our country. We celebrate our troops. We embrace our freedom. We respect our flag. We are proud of our history. We cherish our Constitution, including, by the way, the Second Amendment.

CROWD: USA! USA! USA!

TRUMP: We fully protect religious liberty. We believe in law and order. And we support the incredible men and of law enforcement.

(APPLAUSE)

And we pledge our allegiance to one nation under God.

(APPLAUSE)

You always understood what Washington, D.C. did not. Our movement is a movement built on love. It's love for fellow citizens. It's love for struggling Americans who've been left behind, and love for every American child who deserves a chance to have all of their dreams come true.

TRUMP: From the inner cities to the rural outposts, from the Sun Belt to the Rust Belt, from east to west and north to south, our movement is built on the conviction that every American from every background is entitled to a government that puts their needs first.

(APPLAUSE)

It is finally time to rebuild our country, to take care of our people, and to fight for the jobs our great American workers deserve, and that's what we're doing.

(APPLAUSE)

CROWD: USA! USA! USA!

TRUMP: After our amazing election victory, the forgotten men and women — remember we used to talk about the forgotten men and women before the election? Guess what? They're not forgotten...

(APPLAUSE)

TRUMP: … anymore, right? Anymore. No, they're not forgotten anymore folks. In fact, they're trying to figure you out. They're saying the obstructionists, how do we get them to vote for us? I don't think that's going to happen any time soon.

We believe that every American has the right to live with dignity. Respect for America demands respect for all of its people. Loyalty to our nation requires loyalty to each other, We all share the same home, the same dreams and the same hopes for a better future. A wound inflicted upon one member of our community is a wound inflicted upon us all. You saw last night. You saw last night.

(APPLAUSE)

Did anybody watch last night? Yes.

(APPLAUSE)

When one part of America hurts, we all hurt. And when one American suffers an injustice, all of America suffers together. We're all together.

It's time for us to follow the example of our brave American soldiers. And I was with a lot of them last night, Fort Myers.

(APPLAUSE)

No matter where they come from, no matter what faith they practice, they form a single unbreakable team. That's what we are. We're a team. As a nation, we're a team.

(APPLAUSE)

They're all united by their devotion to our country and to their mission. It's time for all of us to remember that we are all on the same team. We are all Americans, and we all believe right now in America first.

(APPLAUSE)

And it's happening, and it's happening fast. I see all those red hats and white hats. It's all happening very fast. It's called "Make America Great Again." You see what's going on.

(APPLAUSE)

It's coming back, very fast.

We want every child to succeed, every community to prosper and every struggling American to have a chance for a better life. What happened in Charlottesville strikes at the core of America.

And tonight, this entire arena stands united in forceful condemnation of the thugs who perpetrate hatred and violence.

(APPLAUSE)

But the very dishonest media, those people right up there with all the cameras.

(BOOING)

So the — and I mean truly dishonest people in the media and the fake media, they make up stories. They have no sources in many cases. They say "a source says" — there is no such thing. But they don't report the facts. Just like they don't want to report that I spoke out forcefully against hatred, bigotry and violence and strongly condemned the neo-Nazis, the White Supremacists, and the KKK.

(APPLAUSE)

I openly called for unity, healing and love, and they know it because they were all there. So what I did —

(APPLAUSE)

So what I did is I thought, I'd take just a second, and I'm really doing this more than anything else, because you know where my heart is, OK?

(APPLAUSE)

I'm really doing this to show you how damned dishonest these people are.

(BOOING)

So here is my first statement when I heard about Charlottesville — and I have a home in Charlottesville, a lot of people don't know. Here's the first — can't believe they haven't figured that one out yet. Now they know. Now they finally know. But I — I just — I don't want to bore you with this, but I — it shows you how dishonest they are. And most of you know this anyway.

So here's what I said, really fast, here's what I said on Saturday: "We're closely following the terrible events unfolding in Charlottesville, Virginia" — this is me speaking. We condemn in the strongest, possible terms this egregious display of hatred, bigotry and violence." That's me speaking on Saturday.

(APPLAUSE)

Right after the event.

(APPLAUSE)

So I'm condemning the strongest, possible terms, "egregious display," "hatred, bigotry and violence." OK, I think I can't do much better, right? OK. But they didn't want to put this on. They had it on initially, but then one day he talked — he didn't say it fast enough. He didn't do it on time. Why did it take a day? He must be a racist. It took a day.

(BOOING)

Dishonest people. So here is — here is me — I hope they're showing how many people are in this room, but they won't. They don't even do that. The only time they show the crowds is when there's a disrupter or an anarchist in the room. I call them anarchists. Because, believe me, we have plenty of anarchists. They don't want to talk about the anarchists.

So this is me — "it has no place in America." I'm talking about hatred, bigotry and violence. "It has no place in America. What is vital now is a swift restoration of law and order and the protection of innocent lives. No citizen should ever fear for their safety, security in our society, and no child should ever be afraid to go outside and play or be with their parents and have a good time." This is me speaking.

(APPLAUSE)

Here's further. This is on Saturday, the first one. I did this three times. "We have to come together as Americans with love for the nation and true affection, really" — and I say this so strongly — "true affection for each other." I didn't say true affection for you and you. I said for each other, all of us. All of us. All of us.

(APPLAUSE)

But they don't report it. They don't — they just let it go.

"Above all else, we must remember this truth, no matter our color, creed, religion or political party, we are all Americans first. We love our country, we love our God, and we love our flag."

(APPLAUSE)

CROWD: USA! USA! USA!

TRUMP: And then I went on, this is my first statement, and they said, remember they said, well, he wasn't specific enough. Why wasn't he more specific?

So in my second statement, I got really specific, and they said, why didn't he do it faster? The — I'm telling you folks, look, look, I know these people probably better than anybody.

And a lot of people have a problem with it, because look, what happens with them, if they're doing a story about me, I know if it's honest or false.

If you're reading a story about somebody, you don't know. You assume it's honest, because it's like the failing New York Times, which is like so bad. It's so bad.

(BOOING)

Or the Washington Post, which call a lobbying tool for Amazon, OK, that's a lobbying tool for Amazon.

Or CNN, which is so bad and so pathetic, and their ratings are going down.

(BOOING)

Right?

CROWD: CNN sucks! CNN sucks! CNN sucks!

TRUMP: But all the networks — I mean, CNN is really bad, but ABC this morning — I don't watch it much, but I'm watching in the morning, and they have little George Stephanopoulos talking to Nikki Haley, right? Little George.

And — and he talks about the speech I made last night, which believe it or not, got great reviews, right?

(APPLAUSE)

They had a hard time. They were having a hard time because it was with soldiers, we were somber, we were truthful, we were doing — we were saying things — and it really did.

So, he talked about it for like that much, then he goes, "Let's get back to Charlottesville." Charlottesville. And Nikki was great. She's doing a great job, by the way.

So now, I say we have to heal our wounds and the wounds of our country. I love the people of our country, the people, all of the people. It says I love all of the people of our country.

I didn't say I love you because you're black, or I love you because you're white, or I love you because you're from Japan, or you're from China, or you're from Kenya, or you're from Scotland or Sweden. I love all the people of our country.

(APPLAUSE)

So, I said here's my — this is — by the way folks, this is my exact words: "I love all the people of our country. We're going to make America great again, but we're going to make it great for all of the people of the United States of America."

(APPLAUSE)

And then they say, is he a racist? Is he a racist? Then, I did a second one. So then I did a second one.

Don't bother, it's only a single voice. And not a very powerful voice.

How did he get in here? He's supposed to be with the few people outside.

How about — how about all week they're talking about the massive crowds that are going to be outside. Where are they? Well, it's hot out. It is hot. I think it's too warm.

You know, they show up in the helmets and the black masks, and they've got clubs and they've got everything — Antifa!

So on August the 14th — so that was it, and I said all people, I love all people, everything, right? Now I figure I'm going to do it again. I'll be even more specific.

So I said, based on the events that took place over the last weekend in Charlottesville, I'd like to provide the nation with an update. Because that was right after the event, the first one, right?

An update on ongoing federal response to the horrific attack and violence that was witnessed by everybody. To anyone who acted criminally in this weekend's racist violence, you will be held fully accountable, justice will be delivered. That's what I said.

(APPLAUSE)

Listen to that, I said that, but they don't show that. They don't show it. They take — they'll take one thing, like, seriously, he was late was the best thing. He was late.

So I said, to anyone who acted criminally in this weekends racists violence. OK, then I go, we must love each other, show affection for each other, and unite together in condemnation of hatred, bigotry and violence. We must rediscover the bonds of love and loyalty that bring us together as Americans, right?

Then I said, racism is evil. Do they report that I said that racism is evil?

TRUMP: You know why? Because they are very dishonest people. So I said, racism is evil. Now they only choose, you know, like a half a sentence here or there and then they just go on this long rampage, or they put on these real lightweights all around a table that nobody ever heard of, and they all say what a bad guy I am.

But, I mean do you ever see anything — and then you wonder why CNN is doing relatively poorly in the ratings. Because they're putting like seven people all negative on Trump. And they fired Jeffrey Lord, poor Jeffrey. Jeffrey Lord.

I guess he was getting a little fed up, and he was probably fighting back a little bit too hard. They said, we've better get out of here; we can't have that.

And those who cause violence in its name are criminals and thugs, including the KKK, neo-Nazis, white supremacists and other hate groups that are repugnant to everything we hold true as Americans.

Now let me ask you, can it be any better than that, in all fairness?

And you know I mention that, but to the best of my knowledge when there was a big problem, Barack Obama never said it took place because of radical Islamic terrorists, he never said that, right. He doesn't have to say...

(BOOING)

You know why? Because they have a double standard. Because the media is totally dishonest, and they have a double standard. You never heard them say that. And in fact, if you use the term you'd get criticized. But with me, they wanted me to say it, and I said it. And I said it very clearly, but they refused to put it on.

"Those who spread violence in the name of bigotry strike the very core of America." These are my words. This was on Monday, August 14th. So you had Saturday; you had Monday. You know, I was going to do one of these every week, but you would never get it right.

"In times such as these, America has always shown its true character. Responding to hate with love, division with unity, and violence with an unwavering resolve for justice." And then I finished, I said, "We will defend or protect the sacred rights of all Americans." All is capitalized times five. Not just you. "And we will work together so that every citizen — every citizen is free to follow their dreams and their hearts and to express the love and joy in their souls."

(APPLAUSE)

OK now, I mean — so they were having a hard time with that one, because I said everything. I hit him with neo-Nazi. I hit them with everything. I got the white supremacists, the neo-Nazi. I got them all in there, let's say. KKK, we have KKK. I got them all. So they're having a hard time.

So what are they say, right? It should have been sooner. He's a racist. It should have been sooner, OK. So it should have been — so then the last one, on Tuesday — Tuesday I did another one: "We condemn in the strongest possible terms this egregious display of hatred, bigotry and violence. It has no place in America."

(APPLAUSE)

But they also said that he must be a racist because he never mentioned the driver of the car, who is a terrible person, drove the car and he killed Heather, and it's a terrible thing. But they said I didn't mention, so these are my words. "The driver of the car is a murderer, and what he did was a horrible, inexcusable thing." They said I didn't mention it.

And then they asked me, just to finish it, they asked me, what about race relations in the United States? Now I have to say they were pretty bad under Barack Obama, that I can tell you.

But, they asked me the question. And I said, well, I think jobs can have a very big and positive impact. I think if we continue to create jobs like I've done — over one million since I've been in office...

(APPLAUSE)

TRUMP: Way over one million. I think if we continue to create jobs at levels that I'm creating jobs, I think that's going to have a tremendously positive impact on race relations. I do. I do.

And the other thing — very important — I believe wages will start going up, because we now have the lowest unemployment rate we've had in 17 years, so you're going to see wages go up, right?

(APPLAUSE)

They haven't gone up for a long time. I believe wages now, because the economy is doing so well with respect to employment and unemployment, I believe wages will start to go up, and I think that will have a tremendously positive impact on race relations.

(APPLAUSE)

TRUMP: So that was my words.

Now, you know, I was a good student. I always hear about the elite. You know, the elite. They're elite? I went to better schools than they did. I was a better student than they were. I live in a bigger, more beautiful apartment, and I live in the White House, too, which is really great.

(APPLAUSE)

TRUMP: I think — you know what? I think we're the elites. They're not the elites.

(APPLAUSE)

So the point is — and I didn't want to bore you, because you understand where I'm coming from. You people understand. But the point is, that those were three different — there were two statements and one news conference. The words were perfect. They only take out anything they can think of, and for the most part, all they do is complain. But they don't put on those words. And they don't put on me saying those words.

The media can attack me. But where I draw the line is when they attack you, which is what they do. When they attack the decency of our supporters.

(APPLAUSE)

You are honest, hard-working, taxpaying — and by the way, you're overtaxed, but we're going to get your taxes down.

(APPLAUSE)

TRUMP: You're taxpaying Americans who love our nation, obey our laws, and care for our people. It's time to expose the crooked media deceptions, and to challenge the media for their role in fomenting divisions.

(APPLAUSE)

And yes, by the way — and yes, by the way, they are trying to take away our history and our heritage. You see that.

(BOOING)

TRUMP: And — and I say it, and you know, we're all pros. We're all, like, we have a certain sense. We're smart people. These are truly dishonest people. And not all of them. Not all of them. You have some very good reporters. You have some very fair journalists. But for the most part, honestly, these are really, really dishonest people, and they're bad people. And I really think they don't like our country. I really believe that. And I don't believe they're going to change, and that's why I do this. If they would change, I would never say it.

The only people giving a platform to these hate groups is the media itself, and the fake news.

(APPLAUSE) TRUMP: Oh, that's so funny. Look back there, the live red lights. They're turning those suckers off fast out there. They're turning those lights off fast. Like CNN. CNN does not want its falling viewership to watch what I'm saying tonight, I can tell you.

I mean, the advantage I have — the advantage I have is that we do have a big voice. And you know, they're always saying, like Twitter or social media — if I didn't have social media, I wouldn't be able to get the word out. I probably wouldn't be standing here, right? I probably wouldn't be standing here right now.

(APPLAUSE)

If I don't have social media, I probably would not be standing.

And do you ever notice, when I go on and I'll put, like, out a tweet or a couple of tweets, "He's in a Twitter-storm again!" I — I don't do Twitter-storms. You know, you'll put out a little tweet: "I'm going to be with the veterans today." They'll say, "Donald Trump is in a Twitter-storm." These are sick people.

You know the thing I don't understand? You would think — you would think they'd want to make our country great again, and I honestly believe they don't. I honestly believe it.

If you want to discover the source of the division in our country, look no further than the fake news and the crooked media...

(APPLAUSE)

... which would rather get ratings and clicks than tell the truth.

I mean, the New York Times has written some stories. How about this? The New York Times essentially apologized after I won the election, because their coverage was so bad, and it was so wrong, and they were losing so many subscribers that they practically apologized. I would say they did. They say, well, it wasn't really that much of an apology. Because they were losing so many people, because they were misled. And I figured, this is great. And for about two weeks I got good coverage. Then they reverted back into worse than ever before. You know, it's like one of those things.

The Washington Post is terrible. But these are dishonest — but let me tell you, you have some great, honest papers. You have some great networks. I must tell you, Fox has treated me fairly. Fox treated me fairly.

(APPLAUSE)

TRUMP: They've treated me fairly. Hey, I'll let you know. You know what? Some day they might not treat me fairly, and I'll tell you about it, OK? But they've treated me fairly, and I don't mean all good. I get plenty of bad on Fox, too. But at least it's within reason.

And Hannity? How good is Hannity (inaudible)? How good is Hannity?

(APPLAUSE)

TRUMP: And he's a great guy, and he's an honest guy. And "Fox and Friends in the Morning" is the best show, and it's the absolute, most honest show, and it's the show I watch.

Not only does — oh boy, those cameras are going off. Oh, wow. Why don't you just fold them up and take them home? Oh, those cameras are going off. Wow. That's the one thing, they're very nervous to have me on live television, because this can happen.

Now, you know what? I'm a person that wants to tell the truth. I'm an honest person, and what I'm saying, you know is exactly right.

Not only does the media give a platform to hate groups, but the media turns a blind eye to the gang violence on our streets, the failures of our public school, the destruction of our wealth at the hands of the terrible, terrible trade deals made by politicians that should've never been allowed to be politicians.

(APPLAUSE)

And the unaccountable hostility against our incredible police, who work so hard at such a dangerous job.

(APPLAUSE)

My administration is committed to the idea that all Americans have the right to live in safety, security and peace. We believe in the rule of law, because we know that freedom cannot exist if our people are not safe.

And how safe are you at a Trump rally?

(APPLAUSE)

Remember at the beginning, remember when this already started? When this started at the beginning, they used to send in thugs. They had — our people are tougher than them, so it wasn't always very good for them. But they'd send in thugs, and our people would protect themselves, and then you'd go home and you'd watch this violence.

Let me tell you, see this room? You've got people outside, but not very many. But see this room? You're safe in this room. You're very safe in this room.

(APPLAUSE)

It's a big room.

The most sacred duty of government is to protect the lives of its citizens, and that includes securing our borders, and enforcing our immigration laws.

(APPLAUSE) By the way, I'm just curious. Do the people in this room like Sheriff Joe?

(APPLAUSE)

So, was Sheriff Joe convicted for doing his job? That's why...

(APPLAUSE)

He should have had a jury, but you know what? I'll make a prediction. I think he's going to be just fine, OK?

(APPLAUSE)

But — but I won't do it tonight, because I don't want to cause any controversy. Is that OK? All right?

(APPLAUSE)

But Sheriff Joe can feel good. The people of Arizona know the deadly and heartbreaking consequences of illegal immigration, the lost lives, the drugs, the gangs, the cartels, the crisis of smuggling and trafficking. MS-13 — we're throwing them out so fast, they never got thrown out of anything like this. We are liberating towns out on Long Island. We're liberating.

Can you imagine, in this day and age — in this day and age in this country, we are liberating towns. This is like from a different age. We are taking these people. They don't shoot people, because it's too fast and not painful. They cut them up into little pieces. These are animals. We are getting them out of here. We're throwing them in jails, and we're throwing them out of the country. We're liberating our towns.

(APPLAUSE)

You're seen it. You've lived it, and you elected me to put a stop to it. And we are doing a phenomenal job of putting a stop to it. That I can tell you.

(APPLAUSE)

After years of defending other countries borders — can you believe we fight for other countries; we want to defend their borders — we're finally defending our own borders.

(APPLAUSE)

And we're showing compassion for these struggling American workers who are now starting to see the light because plants are coming pouring back into our country.

And by the way, we're doing a lot of good work on that, but a lot of people are coming back in. We have Foxconn, they make the iPhones, as you know, for Apple, and so many companies are building now in our country. (APPLAUSE)

Including the auto companies who are coming back. Years of uncontrolled immigration have placed enormous pressure on the jobs and wages of working families, and they've put great burdens on local schools and hospitals. While this may be good for a handful of special interests, it's unfair to working people of all backgrounds all throughout our country. We want every American community to succeed, including our immigrant communities, but they can't do that if we don't control our borders.

(APPLAUSE)

Earlier today, I visited with the incredible men and women of ICE and the Border Patrol during a visit to Yuma Sector.

TRUMP: I was over at the Yuma Sector. It was hot. It was like 115 degrees. I'm out signing autographs for an hour. I was there. That was a hot day. You learn if you're in shape if you can do that, believe me. And they actually told me — actually, sir, it's relatively cool today. Can you believe that?

(LAUGHTER)

But it was great. And I met with the Border Patrol and I met with ICE, and these are incredible people; the job they do.

(APPLAUSE)

And in fact, General Kelly, who was in charge of Homeland Security, where people coming in down 78 and almost 80 percent. He did so good, I made him my chief of staff, right? That made sense.

John, where's John? Where is he? Where's General Kelly? Get him out here. He's great. He's doing a great job.

But we did a lot before anything happened, we did a lot. We respect and cherish our ICE officers and our Border Patrol agents, and we respect and cherish our police officers, and our firemen, and all of our uniform services.

(APPLAUSE)

But during that visit, I heard first hand from the frontline agents about the security threats they confront each and every day, and I pledged my continued resolve to them, and all of you, to keep our country safe. All around the nation, I have spent time with the wonderful Americans whose children were killed for the simple reason that our government failed to enforce our immigration laws, already existing laws.

And I promised these families, the deaths of their loved ones will not have been in vain. I promised them. I know so many of them.

(APPLAUSE)

One by one we are finding the gang members, the drug dealers and the criminals who prey on our people. We are throwing them out of the country or we're putting the hell, fast in jail.

(APPLAUSE)

We are cracking down on these sanctuary cities that shield criminal aliens, finally.

(APPLAUSE)

And we are building a wall on the southern border which is absolutely necessary.

(APPLAUSE)

CROWD: Build that wall! Build that wall! Build that wall!

TRUMP: Build that wall. Now the obstructionist Democrats would like us not to do it. But believe me, if we have to close down our government, we're building that wall.

Let me be very clear to Democrats in Congress who oppose a border wall and stand in the way of border security: You are putting all of America's safety at risk. You're doing that. You're doing that.

Again, the Border Patrol today, I said, how important is the wall to some of the folks? I met with a lot of them. And they looked at me, they said, it's vital. It's vital. It's so vital. And you know, we have walls. I don't know if you know, we're already starting to fix a lot of the walls we already have, because we don't have to rebuild them. And we want walls that you can see through in a sense. You want to see what's on the other side. But we're starting to fix a lot of the walls. We've done a lot of work.

But I said to them, how are we doing and how important are the walls? And they said, Mr. President, you have no idea. It is desperately needed. We're going to have our wall. We're going to get our wall.

(APPLAUSE)

And that wall is also going to help us, very importantly, with the drug problem, and the massive amounts of drugs that are pouring across the southern border.

(APPLAUSE)

My administration will never back down in demanding immigration control. The American people voted for immigration control. That's one of the reasons I'm here, and that is what the American people deserve, and they're going to get it.

(APPLAUSE)

So you put pressure, but believe me, one way or the other, we're going to get that wall. Immigration security is also a matter, remember this, of national security. That's why we're implementing tough new vetting and screening protocols to keep radical Islamic terrorists out of our country.

(APPLAUSE)

You look at what just happened in Spain and so many other places. Nope. We're really vetting. We're tough. Does anybody want me to be soft on the vetting or would you like —

CROWD: No!

TRUMP: "Extreme vetting" — I came up with that term. That's what it has to be.

So I have a message for Congress tonight: You're job is to represent American families, American people, American workers. That's your job.

(APPLAUSE)

You need to represent them on the border, on taxes, on healthcare — one vote — and on every other issue that affects their lives.

And for our friends in the Senate, oh boy — the Senate, remember this — look, the Senate, we have to get rid of what's called the filibuster rule; we have to. And if we don't, the Republicans will never get anything passed. You're wasting your time. We have to get rid of the filibuster rule. Right now, we need 60 votes and we have 52 Republicans. That means that eight Democrats are controlling all of this legislation. We have over 200 bills.

(BOOING)

And we have to speak to Mitch and we have to speak to everybody.

And I want to tell you, we have some great, great Republican senators. We really do, and they fought like hell to get that thing approved. They fought. They really did. They really fought.

Now, even on healthcare, because of reconciliation, which, if you don't know, it doesn't matter. It's a trick. We needed 51 votes. But when you need 51, and you have 52, and we include the vice president, who always votes with us. He's the greatest. But you have no margin.

But some of the best things in healthcare require 60 votes. So even when you say we're voting on healthcare, like across state lines, purchase across state lines. One of the most important things, I've been talking about it for two years during debates. It gives competition. Insurance companies come in, your prices go way down. Arizona is a disaster in terms of the price increase of your insurance, 116 percent interest.

You got to get rid of the filibuster rule. You've got to go to a majority. You've got to go to 51 votes, and if they don't do that they're — they're just wasting time.

All of the Democrats in Congress, that's the only thing they do well. They do one thing well. You know what it's called? They have no ideas. They have no policies. They obstruct. That's all they do. They're word is, we resist. They don't resist; they obstruct. It's all they're good at. It's all they're good at. That's all they do. On healthcare, they have 48 Democrats. We got no votes. We got no votes. And it would have been great healthcare. And by the way, would have been great healthcare for Arizona. Would have been great.

So the Democrats have no ideas, no policy, no vision for the country other than total socialism and maybe, frankly, a step beyond socialism from what I'm seeing.

(BOOING)

Under they're plan for America, your taxes will double or triple, your service will diminish and your borders will be left wide open for everybody to come in and enjoy our country.

(BOOING)

Obamacare is a disaster and think — think, we were just one vote away from victory after seven years of everybody proclaiming repeal and replace. One vote away. One vote away. We were one vote away. Think of it, seven years the Republicans — and again, you have some great senators, but we were one vote away from repealing it.

(CROWD CHANTING)

But, you know, they all said, Mr. President, your speech was so good last night, please, please, Mr. President don't mention any names. So I won't. I won't. No I won't vote — one vote away, I will not mention any names. Very presidential, isn't' it? Very presidential.

And nobody wants me to talk about your other senator, who's weak on borders, weak on crime, so I won't talk about him.

(BOOING)

Nobody wants me to talk about him. Nobody knows who the hell he is.

And now — see, I haven't' mentioned any names. So now, everybody's happy.

But we are going to get rid of Obamacare. I will never stop — one vote — I will never stop. We're going to get rid of Obamacare.

Every day we're keeping our promises, and that includes our promises to our great, great veterans. Who's a veteran here?

(APPLAUSE)

It's getting better, getting really good. Nobody's fixed it —
nobody's been able to do it. And remember, I'm only here for
less than eight months, you know. When they talk about
Obamacare, it was years. When they talk Hillary Clinton spent
eight years trying to get…

(BOOING)

Eight years trying to get health care.

(CROWD CHANTING)

Well, it's obvious that we won the state of Arizona, do you
agree with that? It's pretty obvious. And we won it by a lot.
And I hear we're winning it by even more right now.

But if you think about it, Clinton, they spent eight years that
they weren't able to get health care. Other administrations spent
all of their time, they weren't able to get it.

Obama, what he did to get it. What he did to get it, including
the guy, Gruber. Did you see Gruber got fired yesterday? He
got fired because he defrauded somebody or something.
Something very bad happened. Check it out. Something
happened.

Gruber, who lied about Obamacare, who called everybody fools
for believing it. Obamacare is gone. It's a disaster. It's gone.
Premiums in other states are going up in numbers that are even
higher than the state of Arizona. Insurance companies are
fleeing, and it's gone.

So we're going to — I really believe that the Republicans — and maybe we'll get a couple of senators that think they're going to lose their race on the Democratic side, maybe, but we'll get it fixed.

One vote — speak to your Senator, please. Speak to your Senator.

We're reforming the V.A. to ensure our veterans have the care they so richly deserve, including choice — choice — choice.

In other words, if you've got to wait for seven days and you're not feeling well, you go see a doctor and we pay for your doctor. Isn't that good? And we've got legislation approved that everybody said was impossible. It's called V.A. Accountability. If somebody treats our veterans badly, we can fire them. We say you're fired; get out of here.

Everybody said — everybody said you couldn't get that — they've been trying to get that passed for 40 years. We got great legislation. You ever hear of these liars back there, where they say, but Trump hasn't gotten — I think we've gotten more in a short period of time, in this seven months, I think we've gotten more than anybody, including Harry Truman, who was number one, but they will tell you we've got none.

So we got V.A. Accountability so that you can fire people that are treating our veterans badly or aren't doing their jobs. Isn't that great?

(APPLAUSE)

We've also obtained historic increase in defense spending to prevent and deter conflict. We believe in peace through strength. We're building up our military like never before.

(APPLAUSE) Thousands and thousands of brave Americans have paid the ultimate price for our freedom. Now it's up to us to preserve and protect their legacy.

Last night, as you know, I laid out my vision for I'm honorable and enduring outcome in a very tough place, a place where country has failed, Afghanistan. This is the place where terrorists are trained, where you have people that are not exactly United States fans, can I say that?

And I will tell you then what we're going to do with our incredible military, they're going to make unbelievable sacrifices, and they've already made, in some cases, the ultimate sacrifice. But we're fighting for them. Our warfighters deserve the tools they need, and the trust they've earned to fight and to win. Fight and to win.

(APPLAUSE)

And you see what's going on in North Korea. All of a sudden, I don't know — who knows. But I can tell you, what I said, that's not strong enough. Some people said it's too strong, it's not strong enough.

But Kim Jong Un, I respect the fact that I believe he is starting to respect us. I respect that fact very much. Respect that fact.

And maybe — probably not — but maybe something positive can come about. They won't tell you that, but maybe something positive can come about.

Every American deserves a government that protects them, honors them, defends them, and fights for them.

And by the way, speaking of that, you have three congressman in the audience and your governor who met me at the plane, and he's now inside, but he said I want to spend my time outside on security. I said, I think that's a great idea, governor. But not that many people showed up so I don't think it should be much of a problem. But you have a hell of a governor, Governor Ducey. You have a great governor.

(APPLAUSE)

And we have three congressman, a friend of mine who has been so great to me, Trent Franks. Where is Congressman Franks? Where is he? Get over here.

(APPLAUSE)

Paul Gosar, Congressman, Congressman Andy Biggs. Get up here, fellow.

Thank you, fellows.

(APPLAUSE)

Thank you, congressman. Never let them go, folks. Never let them go. Don't ever lose them.

Thank you, fellows.

(APPLAUSE)

So, in Washington, we're taking power out of the hands of donors and special interests, and putting that power back into the hands of the people that voted for us, OK? For us. The same failed voices in Washington who opposed our movement are the same people who gave us one terrible trade deal after another; who gave us one foreign policy disaster after another; who sacrificed our sovereignty, our wealth, and our jobs. We don't need advice from the Washington, D.C. swamp.

(BOOING)

We need, right now, to drain the swamp. That's what's happening, too, believe me. Washington is full of people who are only looking out for themselves.

But I don't come to Washington for me. You know, I've had a great life. I've had great success. I've enjoyed my life. Most people think I'm crazy to have done this. And I think they're right. But I enjoy it, because we've made so much — I don't believe that any president — I don't believe that any president has accomplished as much as this president in the first six or seven months. I really don't believe it.

(APPLAUSE)

Including — including a great Supreme Court justice, Justice Gorsuch. Big (inaudible).

(APPLAUSE)

I came to Washington for you. Your dreams are my dreams. Your hopes are my hopes. And your future is what I'm fighting for each and every day. It's so important.

Our agenda is the pro-worker agenda. We've accomplished historic amounts in a short period of time. We've signed more than 50 pieces of legislation. They said we've signed none —

none. We've signed 50; appointed Justice Gorsuch; nominated 31 new federal judges, with many more on the way.

(APPLAUSE)

So, importantly, we have aggressively canceled job-killing regulations, and we're unleashing job-creating American energy like we've never unleashed before.

(APPLAUSE)

We've ended the war on beautiful, clean coal, and it's just been announced that a second, brand-new coal mine, where they're going to take out clean coal — meaning, they're taking out coal. They're going to clean it — is opening in the state of Pennsylvania, the second one.

(APPLAUSE)

And the state of West Virginia, which was way behind and lagging, was now, in terms of GDP increase, second last quarter to the state of Texas. How about that? West Virginia. And they have a great governor in West Virginia, Governor Jim Justice, who just quit the Democrats and joined the Republican Party.

(APPLAUSE)

In the proud tradition of America's great leaders, from George Washington — please, don't take his statue down, please. Please. Does anybody want George Washington's statue? No. Is that sad? Is that all sad? To Lincoln, to Teddy Roosevelt, I see they want to take Teddy Roosevelt's down, too. They're trying to figure out why. They don't know. They're trying to take away our culture. They are trying to take away our history.

TRUMP: And our weak leaders, they do it overnight. These things have been there for 150 years, for 100 years. You go back to a university, and it's gone. Weak, weak people.

We are going to protect American industry. We are going to protect the American worker. No longer will we allow other countries to close our factories, steal our jobs, and drain our wealth. We are building our future with American hands, American labor, American iron, aluminum, and steel.

(APPLAUSE)

We will buy American, and we will hire American.

I immediately withdrew the United States from the disastrous Trans-Pacific Partnership. Would have been a disaster.

(APPLAUSE)

And you know, that one of the worst deals that anybody in history has ever entered into. We have begun formal renegotiation with Mexico and Canada on NAFTA.

(APPLAUSE)

And I must be honest, and I've been talking about NAFTA for a long time, and I'm sorry it's taken six months, but we have to give notice. You have to see this. We have to give notice, and after the notice is given, you have to wait a long time. Then you have to give another one, then you have to wait a long time.

Anyway, we started two days ago, Bob Lighthizer. Personally, I don't think we can make a deal, because we have been so badly taken advantage of/ They have made such great deals, both of the countries, but in particular, Mexico, that I don't think we can make a deal. So I think we'll end up probably terminating NAFTA at some point, OK? Probably.

(APPLAUSE)

But — but I told you from the first day, we will renegotiate NAFTA, or we will terminate NAFTA. I personally don't think you can make a deal without a termination, but we're going to see what happens, OK? You're in — you're in good hands, I can tell you.

We are unleashing American energy, and I withdrew the United States from the job-killing Paris Climate Accord.

(APPLAUSE)

People have no idea how bad that was for this country. Great for other countries. We were like the lap dog. Great for other countries. Our country was so behind.

Since I took the oath of office, we've added far more than one million jobs in the private sector. Unemployment is, right now, at almost a 17-year low. Wages are rising. The stock market is at its all-time high in history, and economic growth has surged to 2.6 percent. Remember, everybody said you won't bring it up to 1 percent. You won't bring it up to 1.2 percent.

And we've just started. Those regulations that we've gotten rid of, which — and we're going to have some regulation, but it's going to be sensible regulation. Those regulations are unleashing our economy.

So we have a GDP, it was shocking, about two weeks ago it was announced for the quarter: 2.6 percent. Remember, I said we're going to try and hit 3 percent? We're already at 2.6. Maybe I'll have to increase my offer.

(APPLAUSE)

And so many of those people, you know, the Economic Council? When it got a little heat with the lies from the media, they sort of said, Oh, we'll take a pass. Not all of them, but some of them did. But I remember the ones that did. But they'll say, We take — oh, we'll take — but people are now calling me, people that have been, like, we'll take a pass — Don, can we get together for lunch? Let's do it privately, instead of through a council. These people just don't get it. They are calling, and they're saying, how about getting together privately? They like it better. Why should they be on a council? You know, that's the way it is, folks. That's the way it is.

To bring more jobs and industry to our shores, we are committed to passing the first major tax reform in over 30 years.

(APPLAUSE)

Now, we need the help of Congress, please. OK? We need the help of Congress. And we really could use some Democrat help. We're giving you the biggest tax cut in the history of our country. The Democrats are going to find a way to obstruct. If they do, remember, they are stopping from getting a massive tax cut. Just remember that, OK? America's crushing business tax is a massive, self-inflicted, economic wound. We have one of the highest business tax rates anywhere in the world, pushing jobs and wealth out of our country.

That is why we are going to lower the tax on American business, to bring back those companies, bring them back to America. We want more products stamped with the letters, "Made in the U.S.A.".

(APPLAUSE)

We also want everyday Americans to be able to keep more of their own money. So for the Democratic senators, especially the ones where I won their states by 20 and 30 points, I really hope you're going to come over to our side. Because again, when you have 52 Republicans, if you lose like two, that's the end. You know what, as good as something is, it's hard to get 51 out of 52.

So I hope some of the Democrats that are going to lose their election will come over and give everybody a big beautiful tax cut, which is going to be great for the economy.

(APPLAUSE)

It's time to pass a tax cut for the middle-class families. We will make America the best place in the world to hire, grow and start a business again. We want to lift our people from welfare to work, from dependence to independence, and from poverty to prosperity.

(APPLAUSE)

We're going to do an infrastructure bill. We will build gleaming new roads, bridges, highways, railways, waterways, all across our beautiful land. Our greatest creations, our most incredible buildings, our most beautiful works of art are just waiting to be brought to life. American hands will build this future. American energy will power this future. We have become an energy exporter for the first time ever just recently.

(APPLAUSE)

And American workers will bring this future to life. We are the nation that dug out the Panama Canal, won two World Wars, put a man on the moon, and defeated communism.

(APPLAUSE)

We can do anything, we can build anything and we can dream anything. It's time to remember what our brave soldiers never forgot. Americans share one flag, one home and one glorious destiny. We live according to the same law, raise our children by the same values, and we are all made by the same Almighty God.

(APPLAUSE)

As long as we remember these truths, as long as we have enough strength and courage in ourselves, then there is no challenge too great, no task too large, no dream beyond our reach. We are Americans, and the future belongs to us. The future belongs to all of you.

(APPLAUSE)

This is our moment. This is our chance. This is our opportunity to recapture our dynasty like never before, to rebuild our future, to deliver justice for every forgotten man and woman and child in America.

Freedom will prevail, our values will endure, our citizens will prosper, Arizona will thrive, and our beloved nation will succeed like never, ever before.

So to Americans young and old, near and far, in cities small and large, we say these words again tonight: We will make America strong again. We will make America wealthy again. We will make America proud again. We will make America safe again. And we will make America great again.

(APPLAUSE)

Thank you Arizona. God bless you. Thank you!